John A Grier

Our Silver Coinage And it's Relation to Debts And the World-Wide Depression in Prices

John A Grier

Our Silver Coinage And it's Relation to Debts And the World-Wide Depression in Prices

ISBN/EAN: 9783744724005

Printed in Europe, USA, Canada, Australia, Japan

Cover: Foto ©ninafisch / pixelio.de

More available books at **www.hansebooks.com**

AND ITS RELATION TO

DEBTS AND THE WORLD-WIDE DEPRESSION IN PRICES.

BY

JOHN A. GRIER,

PHILADELPHIA.

PHILADELPHIA:
PRINTED BY SHERMAN & CO.,
Seventh and Cherry Streets.
1885.

To present an array of statistics and facts on the money question in an attractive way, is no easy task. All I have said has been done carefully and conscientiously. As far as it has been within my reach I have uniformly consulted official records. When my country needed my services in her defence, I tried to do my duty earnestly and to the best of my ability as one of the million; as such of my comrades who are yet living, but scattered all over the world, could testify. Now, as a plain citizen in this monetary emergency, I will try and do my duty, and I have expressed myself freely and fearlessly in defence of my country's honor and her prosperity which are now in great danger. I appeal to the people of our common country to rally around one of our old well-tried measures of value *the silver dollar*, just as we are now all glad to rally around our common flag. This is a contest, in which the poor man as well as the more prosperous is equally interested. Let the men who would be called upon to defend our country against a common enemy wake up, and see if we have not a momentous cause to join hands and hearts against the monetary wreckers and revolutionists of 1873; it matters not what may be their pretensions to financial wisdom or patriotism.

JOHN A. GRIER,
No. 633 N. 40th St.,
Philadelphia.

August 1, 1885.

CONTENTS.

	PAGE
Preface,	3
"Knowledge is wealth, is power, is happiness,"	7
Business depression and the shrinkage in prices. Hard times,	8
Coined full legal standard money, always the measure of intrinsic value,	10
Coined money defined,	11
The amount of silver in our silver dollar never reduced a particle since the first one of 1794,	13
The fineness of coin, and the system of alloy and weight,	16
The Trade Dollar,	19
The coin in the United States not excessive in amount,	20
Mono-metallism and bi-metallism defined,	22
The hostility of the National Banks to the silver coinage,	24
The silver dollar not now worth 100 cents in gold but always worth 100 cents in silver,	27
Gold is not a fixed measure of intrinsic value,	29
The meaning of the word value when applied to money,	30
Coined money the measure, but paper money the principal medium of exchange,	33
Our national debt, including the greenbacks, pledged to be paid in coin, not gold,	36

	PAGE
The effect of the greed of the world for gold,	39
A debt is a contract,	40
Coin obligations of the government payable in silver coin, at the option of the government,	41
Gold payments oppressive, as felt in our panic from 1873 to 1879,	43
Our National Debt,	47
Pensions,	49
Our National Debt as it would appear on wheels,	50
Professor Sumner as an anti-silver advocate,	52
Congress has put a forced legal valuation on gold,	55
An editor's mistake,	57
American Bankers' Association, 1884,	58
The panic of 1873-79,	59
The silver dollar always contains 100 cents,	60
The unit,	65
Custom duties payable in coin,	67
The demonetization of silver in 1873-74 a huge blunder,	68
The effect of the law of 1873 on the unit of value,	69
The clipped gold dollar,	70
The Philadelphia Press,	71
Ernest Seyd and Hon. Wm. D. Kelley,	72
International money and forced valuation,	75
Foreign money not money with us but only metal,	77
Our silver coinage need not drive our gold coins out of circulation,	77
Our gold increasing, not decreasing,	79
The world's production of the precious metals,	81

	PAGE
The amount of gold and silver money in use,	82
Legal tenders,	83
Senator Sherman as a false pilot,	87
Silver bullion certificates based on gold valuation,	89
The pendulum as a measure,	91
The storage of silver dollars,	94
The gold that "nobody wants,"	96
The New York Banks and Clearing House and the silver certificates,	96
Paper money statistics,	98
Opposition of our National Banks to the Silver dollar and Certificates,	98
The business depression abroad,	101
International Monetary Conference of 1881,	101
The Gresham Law,	103
Allison is our Great Magician,	105
Debts due England and Germany by other nations,	106
Practical Bi-metallism,	107
A table of the number owned, percentage of value to the cash in the U. S. Treasury, and cost of the silver in the dollar, from 1879 to 1885,	108

OUR SILVER COINAGE.

"Knowledge is wealth,—is power,—is happiness."

THIS pithy motto placed in golden letters on the wall of one of the old school rooms of my boyhood is distinctly remembered: "Knowledge is wealth,—is power,—is happiness."

Is there any wealth, is there any power, is there any happiness to be obtained from a few hours' patient study concerning some of the fundamental facts in relation to the silver dollar coinage? My object is to mass a few facts on this question, so that a busy, hard-working man may more easily master them, than by searching through official documents, or reading even far more scholarly productions. I will try to give some plainly stated truths, in such straightforward language that more of our busy people, who have no great amount of time nor inclination to study this abstract subject, may have some good reasons for throwing their influence in the right direction on this exceedingly important economic question.

Business depression and the shrinkage in prices.
"Hard-times."

Nations are educated by events, not by arguments. The commercial and industrial depression in prices and in enterprise throughout the civilized world is a matter of sufficient importance to command the close attention and raise the curiosity of nearly every thoughtful person.

This world-wide depression in prices, this world-wide shrinkage of industries are notable events that will educate as no amount of argument can. This derangement in the monetary and industrial affairs of mankind is a sure evidence of some deep-seated economic disease.

It is an inquiry well worthy of the searching examination of the closest thinkers and of the best informed statesmen. The evidences of disease are very apparent; but the causes and the remedies are questions eliciting the most lively and contradictory discussion. Over-production, reckless speculation, action and reaction, intemperance, licentiousness, extravagance, useless expenditure in unjust wars and a thousand other causes are given. Troubles, such as the commercial world is now feeling, cannot justly be attributed to any single cause.

A bullet in the heart of a man is generally a sufficient cause to produce sudden death; so there are economic causes affecting a nation, sometimes severe enough to speedily bring about national extinction. Ordinarily, an individual suffers from a combination of accidents and the common incidents of life, his physical health is wrecked by a hundred causes; so it is with the economic health of the commercial and industrial world. With all of the other chronic afflictions that have been bothering the world, and with which we have been contending, there is a new economic disease that made itself apparent in 1873.

It is the ill-advised attempt *to discard the use of silver as a full legal tender money metal.* After Germany had so successfully conquered France and taken from that country two of her richest provinces, and exacted an indemnity for the cost of the war of over one thousand million dollars, the unification of the German coinage on a gold basis was determined. The law was passed in the latter part of 1871, but was not in a fair way of execution until 1873. From 1857 until this time the sole legal standard of Germany was silver, but then active preparations were made (which, however, have never been fully carried out) to use gold alone for this purpose. In 1873 the United States united with them in this tremendous monetary revolution, without either the statesmen, the financiers, or the people realizing what was being done by the omission of a few words from a new law reorganizing the mints. No provision mas made in that law for the future coinage of the silver dollar which, up to this time, had always been one of our full legal tender coins. Previous to 1853 we had coined over 87 million dollars worth of silver coins, all of which, even the five-cent pieces, were, in the language of the law: "a lawful tender in all payments whatsoever."

The law of Feb. 12, 1873, did not demonetize these old silver coins, although it made no provision for their future coinage; but in the law of 1874, the demonetization was made complete except for the payment of debts not exceeding five dollars. In 1873 this economic disease had a full start by these two great, powerful, commercial and industrial nations of the world, making the public announcement that as for them, they were going to get along in monetary affairs without the use of silver as a full legal tender money metal. Neither one proposed to abandon silver as a subsidiary coin.

Coined full legal standard money always the measure of intrinsic values.

Our object, now, is to study this effect of the attempt to abandon the use of silver as one of the world's well tried standard measures of value. A nation might possibly be prosperous and happy without the use of money metals, but civilized life is so thoroughly wedded to their use that it would be like cutting off the right arms of half the people of the land, to attempt to get along without these metals. During our late war millions of our people did not see a dollar in coin for years; yet our mints were busy in coining, and millions of dollars in accounts were daily settled strictly on a coin basis. During our war years, or the five fiscal years ending June 30, 1865, we coined nearly 174 millions of gold and over 7¾ million dollars worth of silver, of which over six hundred and forty-nine thousand dollars were in silver dollars. We also had a considerable amount of coined money scattered throughout the country, and, although the people at large generally saw but very little of it during the war, it was the real measure of intrinsic value all the time. While coin almost ceased to be the medium of exchange, it measured the approximate value of the greenbacks and the national bank notes in the purchase of commodities and services. As the prospects of a successful ending of the war became brighter or darker, the chances that this representative paper money could be redeemed, in coin, were carefully calculated or rather guessed at, and the prices of all exchangeable commodities rose and fell in obedience to this calculation or guess.

Coined Money Defined

It is rather difficult to define with precision the exact meaning of the word money.

Coined money is a species of common merchandise which—on account of its special fitness for this peculiar duty as an agent of valuation, or as a common measure of intrinsic value, and as a medium of exchange for services or commodities, and for paying legal debts—commands the intervention of statute law in order to certify to its weight and fineness by coinage, and to fix its legal debt-paying value.

The average bullion or intrinsic value of this species of merchandise, coined into full legal tender money, is the common measure of the intrinsic value of all other species of property. It becomes, particularly, the measure of all debts. If the legal money is debased the owner of property, or he who has his services to sell, can raise the price to suit the occasion, but legal debts and legal money go side by side, linked rigidly together. By the Constitution of the United States, Congress has power "to coin money and regulate the value thereof." Hence Congress has full command over all the legal debts in the nation. They have legal power to debase or enrich the full legal tender coin of the country, hence have power to decrease or increase all legal debts. Legal money is purely a creation of statute law.

The Supreme Court of the United States has confirmed, by a late decision, the power exercised by Congress in making our greenbacks full legal tender money for certain debts. This, however, does not entirely settle the question as to the positive distinction between real money and this legal representative money. One of the apparent indispensable requisites to the use of any material as *real* money, is, that on account of some peculiar qualities and fitness it shall approximate, in bullion or intrinsic value, before being coined, to its legal tender value after being coined into money. These requisites are completely filled by both gold and silver. We know that a very great proportion of the bullion value of both gold and silver is justly attributable to this use as money. These metals are specially valuable as bullion, before we as a government may decide to use them as money—simply because if we did not use them, some other nations might do so. The common sense and common usage of mankind have confirmed their use as money for at least twenty-four centuries. But the abandonment of this use of either one of these metals as money by two nations of such commanding influence as Germany and the United States positively did depreciate the intrinsic value of the discarded metal, and increase the intrinsic value of the other. Yet, Senator Sherman, when he was Secretary of the Treasury, in his annual report of 1877, said, with a most remarkable want of knowledge on the subject, "no one did or could foresee the subsequent fall in the market value of silver."

The amount of Silver in our Silver Dollar never reduced a particle since the first one of 1794.

Can we abandon the use of either metal? There are some facts that, when properly represented, are, to my mind, overwhelming in their influence, to cause an ordinary clear-headed man to say that for us to abandon the use of either one of the precious metals as money is an economic crime of gigantic proportions. When the Almighty issued his ten commandments amid the thunders and lightnings of Mount Sinai, He seems to me to have issued one very distinct and positive command against the sin of making a contract to pay a debt, and then repudiating that contract. When He said, "Thou shalt not steal," He seems to tell us, distinctly, that it would be stealing to make great debts, based on being paid either in gold or silver, at the option of the debtor, and then compel the debtor to discard one of these metals and make him pay the debts in the other metal that might be far more difficult to obtain. The fact that the debtor has the option of selecting either metal, shows that it is a great act of injustice to change the contract and take away this option. In order to see into this case, we must refer to the precise details of the United States coinage laws. We must get knowledge; and if we have knowledge, we may have power to use it, and thus we may be of more utility in increasing our wealth, and in fostering our own happiness as well as that of mankind.

The enemies of the silver dollar have asserted most persistently, that it is a debased, a dishonest, a clipped, a light-weight dollar. The simple but positive reply to all of these base libels is an examination of the facts of the case. When you can positively reply that the facts will show, *that the amount of pure silver in our dollar of to-day is exactly the same that it has always been from the first coinage in 1794, until the present time*, the mouths of these libellers should be closed.

There was no change made in the weight of our silver dollar until 1837, when it was reduced from 416 grains to 412½ grains. There was as you will see 3½ grains of copper taken from the weight of each dollar coined after that date. This is the only debasement, this is the only clipping, this is the only light weight that the libellers can show. At the present price of copper, there is about eleven cents' worth, or exactly one pound avoirdupois in weight, taken from every two thousand dollars. Hence, every time you receive two thousand silver dollars for a debt made before the year 1837, you are legally swindled by this coin-clipping Government out of eleven cents' worth of *copper*. But please remember that is according to the Constitution of the United States which gives Congress the power to "coin money and regulate the value thereof." This is the only change that has been made concerning our silver dollar, excepting the one made in 1873 and '74, when its coinage was not provided for by law and its legal tender power was taken away. In 1878, the silver dollar was restored to its old position as a full legal tender for all debts except when otherwise expressly stipulated in the contract.

If a debasement at all, it is such a very small one, that we think you will as freely forgive the Government for it, as you would a tramp who might pull a loose splinter from your fence in order to make a tooth-pick to remove from his teeth a troublesome part of his last free lunch. At that time, even after this debasement, our silver dollars were selling at one per cent. premium over the gold, hence, two thousand dollars in silver were worth about twenty dollars more than two thousand in gold. In 1834, on account of our imperfect system of coinage laws, we could not keep our coined gold at home, as we put fifteen pounds of silver as an equivalent to one pound of gold in our coins. In Europe they used generally fifteen and a half of silver to one of gold. This difference was sufficient under the imperfect coinage laws of that date to make us, as a nation, lose our gold about as fast as it was coined;—hence an alteration in the ratio was made. Congress, in the exercise of its Constitutional rights, reduced the weight of the gold coins in 1834, taking over 6¼ per cent. of pure gold out of each dollar that was coined after that time. In 1837, they added a very small fraction and the gold dollar has remained unchanged from that time. This large reduction of gold in the gold coin was an effort to stand by the silver dollar as a steadier measure of intrinsic value, or unit of valuation, than the gold dollar.

The Fineness of Coin and the System of Alloy and Weight.

It is customary to speak of the fineness of coin expressed in thousands. In both gold and silver coins we now use 900 parts of pure metal to 100 parts of alloy. This is what the inscription 900 fine means that you have doubtless read on the unfortunate trade dollar.

In our first gold coinage we adopted the proportion of alloy used by our mother country, England, which, as they express it, is $\frac{11}{12}$ fine, or as we would express it now, as 916⅔ fine. English standard silver was then, as now, 925 fine. The United States adopted the odd standard of $892\frac{8.9}{208}$ fine for our silver. In 1837, we adopted for both gold and silver, the more elegant and exact decimal, French system of alloy 900 fine. In 1834, we adopted this system for gold very nearly, but accurately in 1837. As most all newly found gold contains some silver, and as it was formerly more troublesome and expensive to drive it all out, the alloy for the gold coins was allowed to contain one-half of its weight in silver and the remainder in copper. Since 1873, only one-tenth of the alloy is allowable of silver. The value of the alloy in coin is so slight as to be practically disregarded.

The total weight of the old standard gold dollar was 27 grains—composed of 24.75 grains of pure gold and 2.25 grains of alloy. The present weight of the standard dollar is 25.8 grains, of which 23.22 is pure gold, 2.58 grains alloy. The former weight of the silver dollar was 416 grains, of the then standard silver, of which 371¼ grains were pure silver and 44¾ grains of alloy or copper. The copper in our dollar since 1837 is, as we have observed before, 3½ grains less, leaving 371¼ grains of pure silver. A cent's worth of copper will furnish enough alloy for about fifteen silver dollars, or about two hundred and fifty gold dollars. This alloy is not put in to add to the weight or value but only to harden the metal and preserve the coin from excessive wear. In 1853, finding that we could not retain in use our small silver coins—(our fifty, twenty-five, ten, and five-cent pieces), the Government gave an opportunity to the people to bring all the old ones that remained in the country to the mint and issued new ones with about six per cent. less silver in them. Since then they have been named subsidiary coins, and were a legal tender for sums not greater than five dollars. Since 1879 they have been a legal tender up to ten dollars. They were no longer money, but became token coins. The changes we have mentioned are all that have been made in the *weight of metal* or *fineness* in our full legal tender coins from the first organization of our mint to the present time. A provision was made in the law of 1834, that any one who had the heavier gold coins could pay them as a legal tender, based on their extra weight.

Legal tender coins have always been based on their *weight* by our laws. If under weight they could always be rejected. The weight, the fineness, the kind of metal, and the stamp of coinage were the four elements that had to be combined to make these coins full legal tender money. This kind of money is not representative of property, but is property, and when paid by the debtor to the creditor, that ends the transaction. But when token money (whether it be silver half-dollars or quarters, or our minor coins, such as the nickel five or three-cent piece, the bronze two or one-cent piece, the greenback or a national bank-note) is paid in the settlement of a debt, the debt is not entirely settled. The Government stands at the back of all its subsidiary silver and minor coins, and makes full provisions for redeeming them in lawful money when presented in definite quantities, at the proper places. Should the Government make this redemption in greenbacks, it again provides to redeem these in full legal tender coin.

The system of debased subsidiary and minor coinage is eminently wise and convenient. There is a constant but ill-advised effort made, however, to have the subsidiary silver coin made equal in intrinsic value to the full legal tender silver dollar. These token coins should always be considered simply as government promissory notes, printed on metal instead of paper. Every reasonable effort should be made, by better coinage, to keep them from being counterfeited. The want of artistic skill and judgment, in making the dies from which these coins are struck, is generally and very justly condemned, and can be vastly improved. They are not money, and do not pretend to be money, although we speak of them in common language, as money. We always speak of the rising and setting of the sun, and speak correctly, but not scientifically. We know that we are understood, but do not mean to say that the sun makes a daily grand round across the face of the sky. These subsidiary and minor coins are very useful as mediums of exchange, and settle small debts legally; but let it not be forgotten that they no more measure debts than the check of a private individual. These small debts, as well as the greater national debts are really measured by the intrinsic value of the full legal tender gold and silver coins that are the real money of the government. As all other forms of money are redeemable in full legal tender coin, this coin becomes the standard or measure of all.

The Trade Dollar.

The Trade Dollar does not concern us much in this present discussion, as it was bullion coined expressly for exportation, yet it was one of the silver coins of the United States, and was a legal tender for over three years and five months, for debts up to five dollars. Nearly 36 millions were coined. Its redemption should have been provided for at its face valuation, when it was demonetized in 1876. Our people should distinctly understand that this redemption was prevented even a few months ago, by the *vote of the anti-silver party in the United States Senate.* The legislation concerning the trade dollar has been bungling and most shameful.

The Coin in the United States not Excessive in Amount.

The stock of coin in our country has never been as great as it is at present. The official estimate of the specie in the United States, in 1852, makes it 204 million dollars; while the official estimate of the specie in our country on June 30, 1884, is 872 million dollars, of which 610 was of gold and 262 in silver. In 1852 our population was about 25 million, hence, while our population has been increasing a little over two and a half times, our specie has increased over fourfold. In 1820, with a population of less than 10 millions, Mr. Gallatin estimated our specie at about 26½ million dollars. Making all just allowances for inaccuracies in such estimates, it is evident that the specie in our country has, of late, increased much more rapidly than our population. Bullion gold and silver, although not real money, yet when in the hands of the government which controls the mint monopoly, are practically money when held in quantities easily coined. The Secretary of the Treasury, in his monthly statements, counts it all as part of the available funds to liquidate debts. Possibly 2½ million silver dollars could be coined in the Philadelphia mint alone, in a single month, by an extra effort, and if this could be done, then it is probable that 2½ million double eagles, making 50 millions in full legal tender gold coin, could be coined there in a single month. Running a mint night and day, however, is not advisable, except in a great emergency; hence the necessity of carrying on the coinage regularly, and without undue haste. The capacity to convert gold into coin so much more rapidly, in case of necessity, than silver, gives gold a most decided advantage over silver as a bullion fund. Of late, the government generally, and most wisely, keeps about 60 millions in gold bullion, and only a few millions in silver. We have coined about 206 million silver dollars since 1878, and about 140 million of them are represented by silver certificates. France, with a population of about 38 million, has over 537 million dollars' worth of full legal tender silver in circulation. Our 206 million silver dollars does not seem excessive for our probable 57 million people.

The hue and cry that many intelligent people make about the useless coinage of silver dollars, that "nobody wants," and that are only made to clog up the government vaults, will not bear critical examination. We will find that these dollars are doing us good service, although quietly buried and resting in these steel-clad vaults. Every silver dollar coined will honestly and equitably pay one dollar of debt. Every silver dollar that is coined, has a tendency to reduce the burden of all debts. Every silver dollar coined has a tendency to reduce the demand for gold, and hence reduce its bullion value when compared to silver.

The remonetization of silver, and its continued coinage, has removed this metal from the second-rate position in which it was placed in the year 1873, as far as we, as a nation, are able to replace it by our laws. It again becomes one of our money-metals, and is doing duty as one of the measures of all of the debts, as well as of all of the property in our country. We cannot make laws, however, for the remainder of the world, but we can set a good example, and throw our influence in a right direction.

Mono-metallism and Bi-metallism Defined.

In this discussion, there are two terms often used which should be understood: *mono-metallism*, which, as its derivation indicates, is the use of one of the precious metals as full legal tender money; while *bi-metallism* means the use of both metals. Everywhere, to a certain extent, both metals are used as money. Great Britain is said to be a gold monometallic nation at home, because gold is the sole standard of value, yet in her large empire of India, with her 237 million subjects, she is silver monometallic, as over 1000 million dollars' worth of full legal tender silver is used there. A debt cannot be paid in India legally, in gold. In England about 95 million dollars' worth of silver is estimated to be in circulation, but it is a legal tender only to the amount of forty shillings or less. It is, however, the money of the common people generally. We have more gold than Great Britain.

The statement is made in the Congressional report of the Monetary Commission of 1877 that the population of the mono-metallic silver countries is about 770 millions; while the mono-metallic gold countries is about 93 millions. At that time the bi-metallic countries numbered 137 millions; to these we can now add our people, and we might say that 190 millions are now under the bi-metallic flag. Hence, those who used silver exclusively as their money standard or used it concurrently with gold, exceed those who use gold alone as a standard in the proportion of over ten to one. Some more recent statistics change these figures, yet the evidence is full and conclusive that gold is not the money of the world. We may estimate the rest of the people of the world as uncivilized, transacting their affairs by barter.

There are but few subjects the influence of which extends more positively over every hour of productive labor, to *every man's home* and possessions in this broad land, that has received less careful examination and is less understood than this money question. We, the people, must take hold of this silver question, and those who are patient enough to devote some earnest thinking on the subject, must make their influence felt at Washington. The Congress that will handle this question for the next two years is elected. The strongest kind of influence will be brought to bear in favor of the immediate stoppage of the silver coinage. Public sentiment is frequently felt very positively, even at times when there is no opportunity to express that sentiment by the ballot; it should therefore be aroused. As about 45 per cent. of the money of the world consists of silver, and about 55 per cent. of gold, we see the commercial world standing face to face with one of the most colossal crimes of this or of any other age, when we see the efforts made to discard nearly one-half of the full legal tender money metals of the world. This monetary revolution has been led by exceedingly able, but we believe, misguided men. Authorities, deservedly ranking high in the estimation of the people, can be quoted largely for either side. The time seems to have arrived when this question of the continued use of both silver and gold as full legal tender money metals must be decided by the people in their sovereign capacity.

During the last Presidential and Congressional election the question was generally suppressed. Neither the platforms nor the letters of acceptance of either of the two leading political parties gave a clue as to how the party or the candidates stood. It was declared not to be a party question. In fact, the question was cunningly evaded by both parties, expressly, we believe, on account of its vital importance.

The hostility of the National Banks to the silver coinage.

The national banks of the United States have been particularly outspoken on the subject ever since the coinage law has been passed. We know their general views and are utterly opposed to their method of thinking, believing it to be selfish and exceedingly impolitic and unwise, even for their own good. Mr. George S. Coe, President of the American Exchange National Bank of New York City (a very able and prominent gentleman), expressed, in a few words, the sentiments of many at the Bankers' National Convention, held at Louisville, Ky., in Oct., 1883. It was reported in the newspapers of the day that when he was foretelling the mischief that would probably be made by this continued silver coinage, he said: "that rather than have the outrage continue that it would be better that the whole amount of these rejected dollars that now encumber the Treasury vaults should be sunk in the sea." Do not get angry at such remarks. If a blind man runs against you on the street and yet insists on his being able to see, you are patient. Would you whip a young colt because he is afraid of a buffalo robe? When the streets become full of blind men we must be more careful of our own movements.

Even since 1878 there has been one long, unending howl from a large and influential class of people threatening bankruptcy and ruin from this silver coinage and an utter destruction of national honor and credit. These false prophets are still wailing. Their prophecies have not yet been fulfilled, but they continually cry "wait and you will see!" We have great financial troubles, but our national credit is not suffering. *It is the best in the world.* The financial troubles from which we suffer are world-wide and so has been the effect of the partial discarding of silver as a money metal. We connect this particular cause with this effect. The feeble attempt of the United States to again use silver freely has not yet and cannot counteract the bad effect of the anti-silver agitation throughout the remainder of the commercial world. We have not coined enough. We have not shown a bold, manly example on the silver question.

The national executive administration and a large proportion of our leading newspapers have been bitterly and constantly hostile to the silver coinage. When Secretary Sherman, of the Treasury, in his Annual Report of 1879, taught that it was not a full honest dollar, he sounded the official key-note that has never ceased to ring. Although our national platform and the speeches and letters of the two leading parties were a complete blank on the question, President Cleveland had not yet taken his seat when he issued an anti-silver coinage letter that has opened up the entire question. This letter was ably answered by the friends of silver in Congress. Should the wishes of the anti-silver men be successful, a tendency to a further increase in the demand for gold, a further decrease in prices, a tendency to a further depression of business is, we think, inevitable. Even the marked position of the President on the silver question, we believe, causes a further decline and depression in our domestic affairs; and until the matter is adjusted by the decided action of the next Congress in favor of the continued coinage of silver, we fear that the effect will be injurious.

The gold men are in fairly good spirits and count largely on the divisions among the old friends of silver. The bi-metallists are sadly divided. Many who advocated the silver dollar law of 1878 are now anxious to stop the coinage until we can obtain the coöperation of more foreign nations, and some think we have coined enough, as our vaults are becoming too crowded to suit their ideas. Many of the mono-metallists would be satisfied if the plan of the issue of silver certificates based on the bullion value of silver measured by gold would be adopted. In fact, this plan is fathered by one of the leading friends of silver in the House of Representatives, Hon. A. J. Warner, of Ohio.

The silver dollar not now worth 100 cents in gold, but always worth 100 cents in silver.

We have shown that our silver dollar is not a clipped or light weight dollar. We are constantly told, however, that it is not worth one hundred cents in gold, and we admit that it is worth as bullion, at present, only a little less than 83 cents in gold. This is a point that deserves the fairest kind of a reply, and if it is found that either nature or the law of man has made gold a true, unvarying standard of intrinsic value, then our Government, perfectly regardless of other serious consequences, would be wise in selecting it as our sole standard. But please remember that gold, like silver, is one of the common commodities of life and its intrinsic value is subjected to exactly the same rigid economic law of supply and demand. This truth is taught everywhere and by everybody who has the least weight in political economy. The entire weight of all scientific economists is distinctly thrown to the side, showing that there is no fixed measure of intrinsic value. When you hear that a well-known Philadelphia orator, in making an address to Philadelphia merchants on this subject, in 1880 (one whom some of our local newspapers were accustomed to quote as the highest authority on coinage), spoke of gold as "an unvarying yard-stick," as "the true measure of value," "as fixed as the North Star,"—be on your guard against pretense to science, not knowledge.

In fact, this is not a question a clear-headed, thinking man would ask of a political economist. A fair disinterested man, with a low classed brain power, should see plainly that if the supply of gold became very great and the demand but little, it would soon become much cheaper.

It is one of the pivotal points of this entire question that gold *has not a fixed intrinsic value;* that gold is not a true unvarying measure of intrinsic value. Neither is silver, nor are they both combined, unvarying measures of intrinsic value. Either one would be an *elastic* standard, and both together are necessarily *elastic standards.* But what the entire commercial world wants, and imperatively demands, is some standard of intrinsic value that will vary *less* than any other. This, we claim, has been given to us, by the concurrent use as money, of these two precious metals, by man as far back as we can go in historical records.

Can we compare gold as a measure of intrinsic value to a yard-stick as a measure of length, or to a bushel as a measure of capacity? Yet this is constantly done by people who misunderstand the whole question. You will see this done by careless thinkers on such subjects, but never by exact scientific scholars. The entire subject of weights and measures has always demanded the closest attention of some of the keenest intellects of every age. Lose all the yard-sticks in the world, lose all of our standard weights, lose all the measures of capacity, and we can refer to the unvarying laws of gravity, and from the swing of a pendulum and the rotation of the earth on its axis again obtain these measures. The swing of a pendulum under certain fixed conditions is as unvarying as the rotation of the earth on its axis. These are fixed measures that are unvarying. What nonsense it is, then, to compare with such measures, the fixity of intrinsic or bullion value of a metal like gold, the annual supply of which has varied eighteenfold in the present century! It is the commanding and most delusive fallacy of this entire question.

Gold is not a Fixed Measure of Intrinsic Value.

Professor W. Stanley Jevons, an English authority of the highest reputation as a scientific financier and statistician, in his valuable work on "Money" tells us that "from 1809 to 1849, a period of only forty years," gold raised in intrinsic value 145 per cent. Or, in other words, prices of the average commodities in use in England during that period fell about

60 per cent. measured by gold. This means, that during these 40 years, gold was getting scarcer and dearer on account of the extraordinary demands made for real money by the increasing commercial and industrial activity of the world. This was equally true of silver, as for the first 73 years of this century, on account of the world's practical bi-metallism, particularly in France, the intrinsic value of gold and silver, when compared with each other, varied but a trifle. After 1849, came the immense flood of gold from California and Australia, reaching its height in California in 1853, and in Australia in 1856. Notwithstanding this immense supply of gold on the markets of the world the practical bi-metallism of the commercial world absorbed it all, setting silver free and maintaining the equilibrium in the relative intrinsic value of these metals. Coined money became cheaper, or in other words, prices of labor and the products of labor rose, debts remained the same, measured by dollars or francs, but the burden of debt was greatly lightened on the backs of the producer and taxpayer.

Is it not evident that the intrinsic value of the full legal tender coins measured by debts or commodities varied greatly during this period? Use your own judgment and do not refer to others to think for you on a question so simple and yet so important.

The Meaning of the Word Value, when applied to Money.

There is a fallacy lurking under the use of the term " value," when applied to the word money, to which I wish particularly, to call your attention. This term "value" should be qualified either by two distinct words, or by its surroundings, in order to be understood. For instance, an English pound sterling had the debt paying value of one pound from 1809 to 1849. Yet, Professor Jevons tells us that it would purchase about 145 per cent. more of the articles generally used in common life in 1849 than in 1809. The legal debt paying value of the coined pound remained unvarying, fixed; while the purchasing or exchangeable value increased in this surprising ratio. The statute law fixed the weight, the fineness and the debt paying value of the pound sterling; but here the statute law stops, as it always must in a free country, and the people, independent of statute law, will regulate prices. In the midst of our darkest greenback days a dollar greenback might not have been worth more than 38 cents in gold, or $39\frac{1}{2}$ cents in silver, yet it would pay an ordinary legal debt equally as well as either of the coined dollars. This was the debt paying value fixed by statute law. Go into our markets and you could buy more articles with the gold dollar and three per cent. more with our silver dollar, but the legal debt paying value of each of these coin dollars was only equal to the debased greenback.

The legal tender value of the money of a nation is a very serious matter to trifle with, and should never be touched except in the most serious emergency or for a very sound reason. Our Government has kept faith with the people in our coined money with great credit. The change in the debasement of ten and a half cents (the price of copper now) in every two thousand dollars of silver coined after 1837, and the deduction of about $6\frac{1}{4}$ per cent. from the gold coined after 1834, has been the only tampering with the full legal tender coins until the year 1873. As Congress has the constitutional power to make these changes and had good reasons for them, we cannot justly find fault.

It has been said that if, when we made the change, in 1834, of altering our ratio from 15 lbs. of silver to 1 lb. of gold—to our present ratio of nearly 16 lbs. of silver to 1 lb. of gold,—had we then adopted the general European ratio of $15\frac{1}{2}$ to 1, it is probable that this ratio would have been adopted by this time as an international ratio greatly to the benefit of the commercial world. Having adopted our independent ratio, we can not easily nor wisely drop it under the present accumulated load of debts which it measures. During the four fiscal years ending June 30, 1865, or, as we may call them, our war years, the average value of the silver in the silver dollar is officially stated to be about $3\frac{3}{4}$ per cent. greater than the value of the bullion in the gold dollar. In these years about eighty-nine thousand silver dollars were coined, notwithstanding this difference in the market price of bullion. There was quite a large amount of subsidiary silver coined also, but it did not get into the hands of the people, except on the Pacific coast, where coin was used in general, during our greenback days. Previous to 1857 certain foreign silver coins were a legal tender at a rate fixed by the Government, and Spanish, Mexican, and other silver dollars filled the place that should have been filled by our own coins. The use of this foreign money was then quite extensive. There is no disputing the fact that the great bulk of our large coin payments, of late years at least, have been made in gold and not in silver.

In round numbers, our mints have coined since their establishment, about 1400 millions of gold, and only about 434 millions of silver. Previous to 1873, of all this immense sum, we coined but little over 8 million silver dollars. As about 87 million dollars was coined in silver money,—when all silver was "a lawful tender in all payments whatsoever," and about 5¼ million silver dollars were coined after 1853 to 1873, and about 206 since 1878,—we can see that about 298 million of all the silver that has been coined has been a full legal tender in all payments excepting from 1873 to 1878. So silver *has played a very important part in the full legal tender money of the United States.* When the false assertion is made that gold alone, unaffected by silver, measured the value of debts and exchanges, we must utter a most decided protest. The measuring of the intrinsic value of commodities or services, done by full legal tender coined money, is a duty performed by this money that should never be lost sight of for a moment.

Coined Money the Measure, but Paper Money the Principal Medium of Exchange.

On June 30th, 1880, the then Comptroller of the Currency, Hon. John J. Knox, received the statistics of that day's work in nearly two thousand of our National Banks. A business on that day is reported of nearly 274 million dollars, but less than one per cent. of this entire business was done by coined money, including gold, silver, and minor coins. What percentage of this was caused by the token coined money for the sake of making small change, is not noted. Is there any reason to doubt that, although over 99 per cent. of this immense business was transacted by means of some of the various kinds of representative money, that the intrinsic value of the full legal tender gold and silver coins did not regulate or measure the entire business? Unless you can grasp the idea clearly—that the most important function of full legal tender gold and silver money is to measure the intrinsic value of everything—while its minor function is to act as a medium of exchange for commodities and services, I fear that the study of this little book will not be satisfactory.

All the property of the civilized world—all the debts of the civilized world—are measured by the bullion value of the metals used as full legal tender money. When a legal debt has to be paid, and the bullion value of the money metal has been increased from any cause, either by the diminished supply, or increased demand, the debt becomes really larger, yet it will still be named as so many dollars, pounds, francs, marks, or by whatever may be the name of the national money of accounts.

Gold and silver together have done this measuring, and this tremendous monetary revolution so unfairly started in 1873, is making an effort to discard silver from this important duty.

With charity towards others who may think differently, but feeling as I do on this subject, I would shrink with as much reluctance from aiding or abetting such an infamous scheme, as I would from deliberately putting a deadly and insidious poison in a river furnishing a city of a million inhabitants with its drinking water. It is no small crime to assist to wreck the social and financial happiness of hundreds of millions of people, by thus unsettling the value of the accumulated wealth of ages, and of almost doubling the vast amount of legal debts of the world. A man or nation will righteously defend property as courageously as they will life. I speak strongly, because I feel earnestly as one whose heart is in sympathy with human sufferings and human struggles. Double the debts of the world, and decrease by one half the value of accumulated labor, and a wrong would be committed, of which no one, unless he was an enemy of the human race, would wish to be accused. This is what, we believe, the entire discarding of silver as a full legal tender money metal would do, and is what the partial discarding of silver has a constant tendency to do.

It is a revolution undertaken by these false monetary reformers to which the attention of the mass of our people—we who do the voting and the fighting—should be turned by the strongest possible language. It is a question in which the people have an immense interest at stake, and yet, I am sorry to say, they have given it comparatively but little attention, thinking it is a question of no importance to them; they seem willing to let the bankers and politicians talk and quarrel over it without their advice or influence.

Our National Debt, including the Greenback, Pledged to be Paid in Coin, not Gold.

Our great national debt was contracted to be paid in *coin*. At the time when this debt was contracted, and until 1873, as I have shown, there can be no possible dispute, nor reasonable question, as to what a coined dollar meant under the laws of the United States. We had two: the one of standard gold, weighing 25.8 grains; the other of standard silver, weighing 412½ grains. The exact fineness of these standards was clearly defined in our laws. They were each an unlimited legal tender for all debts, public and private, unless otherwise specified. They were each regularly coined at our mints. We are happily governed as a nation by written laws, and not by the whim of an irresponsible ruler.

The example of that great brainy nation, Germany does not justify us in changing our laws in regard to our money metals. Perhaps, when the Germans find out the exact cause of nearly a quarter of a million of their people annually tearing themselves from their native land, they may find this partial discarding of silver had more to do with giving them long hours of labor, coarse food and general poverty, than they will now admit.

Perhaps, if our English cousins knew everything,

they might find that the miserable times that are recorded during the first twenty-five years after the close of the Napoleonic wars, and after the partial discarding of silver in 1816, were due in a greater degree to this cause, than they now suppose. The records of those fearful years in the history of the common people of Great Britain, are an ugly blot on their boasted intelligence, civilization, and professed Christianity. Augustus Mongredien tells us, in his little history of "The Free Trade Movement in Great Britain," that in 1841, in the city of Leeds, there were nearly 21,000 people whose average earnings were less than twenty-five cents a week, while wheat cost about one dollar and eighty-eight cents a bushel, with an average protective duty of seventy-five cents a bushel. Let any of our people who may complain of "hard times" and yet turn to England for financial wisdom, think of facts like these, and thank God that they live in better times and under a wiser government. This was, he assures us, only a representative case, while all through the country there was the same kind of distress. He justly blames this distress on the infamous system of "protective tariff," as they foolishly called their duty on grain, or Corn-Laws. Other historians tell us of the miserable condition of commercial and industrial affairs after 1816, when silver was discarded as a full legal tender money, and the great war debts, as well as private debts, based on both metals, had to be paid or adjusted on the basis of gold alone. Mortgages by the hundreds, given for one-third or one-half of the purchasing price of property, became the deeds to the entire property. They had the same kind of a monetary struggle that we had in getting down from a paper basis to a coin basis. We believe that their paper money never got below a discount of 41 per cent., while ours struck about 64 per cent. In our darkest days we quoted gold at 284. We had a hard pull in getting down towards a coin basis up to 1873, but this struggle was greatly intensified in our attempt to get down to a *gold* coin basis from 1873 to 1878.

This gold legislation, doubtless, greatly intensified the grievous burdens of the Southern States during those very troublesome years. It greatly injured their restoration to prosperity, and did an immense amount of harm.

Do not let us turn to either Germany or England, and accept all they may try to teach us, as the quintessence of financial wisdom. National distress is not generally caused by one mistake in government, but a grave financial mistake will always be a most fruitful cause of misery. The discarding of silver as a full legal tender money metal in 1816 by Great Britain, and partially by Germany in 1871, has not produced all the distress it would have done if all other civilized nations had followed their example. France, by her financial sagacity, has particularly acted as the great international balance-wheel, maintaining, for the first seventy-three years of this century, a comparative equilibrium in the intrinsic value of silver and gold. In self-defence she wisely closed her mints against silver in 1876, and has kept them closed ever since. As we have seen, she is abundantly stocked with full legal standard silver money.

The effect of the Greed of the World for Gold.

Is it not most evident that a fierce legislative grabbing for gold among all the civilized nations of the world will make gold scarcer and dearer? When we say gold is dearer, it simply means that it will require more of the products of human labor, or more days' labor to procure a definite quantity of gold, or its equivalent in paper money, to pay debts. Should a farmer have a mortgage against his farm, it means that he must raise more grain or other products to obtain the money to pay either his interest or the principal of his debt. The debt may remain exactly the same measured by dollars, but the burden of paying the debt may be doubled by the coin becoming twice as dear as it was when the mortgage was given.

A thoughtless person may say, that as he has no debts, the silver question is of no interest to him. No one, unless he is a dependent or a pauper, can live in a civilized community without sharing in the payment of the debts of that community and of the nation. In fact, the hard working and poorly paid day laborer feels his portion of taxation more severely than the prosperous business man. He may never see a tax-collector, indirectly he has much less tax to pay, but paying that little, deprives him and his family of certain much desired comforts or necessaries.

A Debt: a Contract.

It is the desire of all honest men to pay their debts as agreed upon, if possible. Every debt made payable in money at a future date is a contract. This contract does not guarantee the intrinsic value of the money that is to be paid. In other words, the contract does not guarantee the price of commodities when the debt becomes due. The government that makes the statute law for the collection of this debt and for its payment in money, when due, has no strict moral right to alter the money of the contract until the debt is paid. This is exactly what our government did, when, in 1873, it put it out of the power of the people to pay either the principal or interest of the public or private debts in silver coin. It was well to remedy this great wrong of 1873 in 1878.

There are thousands of intelligent people who erroneously think that we would dishonor ourselves if we should pay any part of this debt in silver dollars. They seemingly forget the history of the silver coinage of our nation. They forget that this question was settled in 1869, long after the war was over, and when certain people were advocating the policy, with a great show of argument, that the way to pay an old debt was to make a new promise to pay it. By the act of Congress passed March 18th, 1869, it was solemnly promised that in order to remove any doubt as to the purpose of the government in this matter, all just obligations were pledged to be paid in coin, or its equivalent, except when otherwise provided. The redemption of the greenback in coin, "at the earliest practical period," was also pledged in this same law. Let it be remembered, that the word in the law is "*coin*," not gold, not silver, but coin, and we had two kinds of full legal tender coin —gold and silver. Would it not be well then to promptly commence this redemption, and issue one and two dollar silver certificates in the place of all the one and two dollar greenbacks?

Coin obligations of the Government payable in silver coin at the option of the Government.

It is said that the average amount of coin paid for our dollar bonds was only about 57 cents. We accept the contract as perfectly fair and are willing to return one dollar in coin for each, together with the interest in coin until they are paid. At present it is just as convenient for the Government to pay coined gold as it is to pay coined silver, and let the Government take its option. The day may come, and, in fact, looks as if it were getting near when the Government may see fit to use some of its silver in paying coin obligations. Be assured, if that day does come, the Government is under no more of an obligation, either by law or in equity, to pay the bond-holders in gold coin than you would be if you at this time employed a man to do a piece of work for a dollar and you would pay him in silver. He might know that you had plenty of gold, or if you did not have it that you could well afford to get it, and demand that you pay him in gold. He might very unjustly denounce you as a scoundrel because you did not and would not pay him in gold.

On July 12, 1882, a law was passed requiring the Government to stop the issue of gold certificates whenever the amount of gold in the Treasury reserved for the redemption of United States notes fell below 100 million dollars. This was simply an acknowledgment by the Government that the Treasury notes (greenbacks) were a coin debt and that this amount of coin was reserved as security for their payment. Should the Secretary of the Treasury have any other full legal tender coin at his command and greenbacks were presented for payment, it is entirely optional with him by law to redeem all of these greenbacks with either gold or silver. The gold is there as part security that they will be redeemed in coin, but that is no reason that this kind of coin *must* be paid. Should you borrow fifty dollars and deposit your hundred dollar watch as security, when you pay the fifty dollars legally, your claim for the return of the watch is complete. The greenbacks were, in a measure, a forced loan made by the people to the Government, which loan is not yet paid and the people are now so well satisfied with it that they do not demand its immediate repayment, and the Government shows its ability to pay it when demanded and has wisely made provision to meet all probable legal demands.

Gold payments oppressive, as felt in our Panic from 1873 to 1879.

Do you recall the incident that when we, as a nation, were particularly squeezed under the mono-metallic thumb-screw during the six financial famine years ending June 30, 1879, that with our united energies as a nation we paid off our national debt at the slow rate of only about twenty million dollars a year? I do not attribute this evident national weakness during those years to this gold mono-metallism alone, but I believe it was the leading and treacherous cause at the bottom of our troubles prolonging and intensifying that uncomfortable panic from 1873 to 1879. Soon after the remonetization of silver coinage in 1878 we had a spurt for a few years of fairly good times, caused in part by our excellent harvests and the correspondingly bad ones of Europe.

Although we are one of the most powerful and influential nations of the world, we depend to a large extent on a thrifty world beyond the seas to market our surplus products. This extraordinary greed for gold has increased the demand for it, and as gold plays such an important part in measuring the value of our products abroad, these products when sold bring us less money. This world-wide depression in prices is caused by this new legislative greed, and in turn the depression in prices has discouraged the leaders of great industries from going ahead with their accustomed energy or has prevented them from starting new enterprises on a falling market.

The financial world is sick, very sick. Is it not

plausible that this sickness in a great measure is traceable to this comparatively new cause, the partial discarding of silver as one of the principal money metals of the commercial world? When this monetary revolution is settled there are plenty of other mischief-making causes that will probably keep us from enjoying the millenium.

Although we want a thrifty world in order to sell our surplus products, such are the unexampled capabilities of our own magnificent country that we have it in our power by a declaration of industrial independence to enjoy as much, if not more, of the blessings of life than any country under the sun. Besides the many things in demand from legislation we especially demand a sound financial system, and an abundant currency worth 100 cents on the dollar, at all times redeemable in coin.

In this age of the rapid advance of physical science, steam, electricity and labor-saving machinery, we have been making most wonderful progress in commercial and industrial activity. The annual supply of gold to the world is *decreasing*, while that of silver is *very slightly increasing*. From these reasons it is not improbable that a debt payable in gold alone, thirty years hence, may increase wonderfully in intrinsic value, unless this value is regulated by bimetallism. Bearing in mind the new demand for gold and our *decreasing* supply, every effort that we make to reduce its importance as a money metal by the use of silver has a constant tendency to decrease the intrinsic value of gold and increase the intrinsic value of silver.

Extraordinary efforts have been made by men of great breadth of intellect and influence in the respective countries of Germany and Great Britian to persuade them to again remonetize silver. So far these efforts have been failures. But the melting up and sale of the German stock of silver ceased in 1879, after a direct loss to that Government of over 17 million dollars. It is said that there are over 150 million of these German silver thalers still left doing full duty as full legal tender money. Bismarck found fault with his Minister of Finance, Delbrüch, and intimated very plainly that a mistake was made in their haste to change the basis of all debts. Revolutions go slowly, especially backwards. Even now the Imperial Bank of Germany holds three times more silver than gold as its legal reserve for its notes.

There is a large and influential class of theoretical bi-metallists, as we may courteously call them, in our country who strongly advocate the stoppage of the silver dollar coinage in order to hasten a financial crisis in these countries across the seas, so that they will be compelled by threatened bankruptcy and ruin to comply with our wishes in this respect. I feel afraid of the influence of these dubious friends of silver, and cannot understand their reasoning nor sympathize with their plans. While a stoppage of our silver coinage would probably do considerable financial mischief to both England and Germany, I fear greater mischief at home. It is like sinking our ship in order to get rid of rats.

We have a serious duty as one of the most influential nations of the earth to perform. We are right in setting a good example in stemming this revolution by coining full legal tender silver, and need the silver to give greater stability to our financial situation and to reduce the burden of our legal debts. The mistake we have made is in not working our mints to their full capacity ever since the silver law was enacted. We should at least have absorbed all of our domestic production of silver. During the last few years we have exported about 12 million dollars' worth of silver annually.

I care nothing in particular for the prosperity of our silver producers. They deserve no more nor less consideration than the producers of any of the other commodities of life. Most of them ask no favors, but they want fair play. They are not like the manufacturers of heavy guns or first class steamships. These, are essential for national protection and independence; the silver producers are not. They are a laborious and most worthy class of pioneer citizens and are doing most excellent service in enriching the world and in opening up our wild western lands. I would advocate the continued and even the increased coinage of silver, even if we did not produce an ounce of it in our country. Every dollar coined will pay one dollar of our national debt honestly and equitably. Every dollar adds to our national prosperity. Every dollar tends to increase the value, measured by dollars, of a day's labor, and most justly decrease the burdens of all legal debts. We cannot probably get other nations to re-coin their money to suit our ratio, and we cannot change our ratio to theirs without a breach of contract. It is worth while for you to take a good, square look at this national debt and see how we are handling it.

Our National Debt.

On August 1, 1865, in round numbers, our National debt was 2756 million dollars, after deducting the entire amount of cash in the United States Treasury. On June 30, 1885, it was 1485 million dollars, after deducting all the cash in the treasury. Hence, we have paid off about 1271 million dollars during these twenty years. This is a large sum—do you realize what it means? It has been a payment of over $7,250. for every hour, day and night, for twenty years. In addition during these twenty years we have paid off about 1890 million dollars in interest on this debt. This means nearly $11,000. paid out every hour, day and night, for twenty years in interest. With all this enormous outlay, of which we as a nation are justly proud, we are startled with the information that our debt is larger now than when we thought it was the largest in 1865. In dollars it is smaller, but measured by cotton or bar iron, two of the leading products of human labor in our country, it is *larger*. The products of human labor to-day are so cheap when compared to the prices of 1865 in gold, that it is a fact, that measured by a large number of articles, the debt has increased.

The silver advocates in Congress, on March 1, of this year, in reply to President Cleveland's anti-silver coinage letter, make the statement, on their own calculations—that 18 million bales of cotton would have paid the debt in 1865, while it would take 35 millions to do it now, although so much decreased. They also say 25 million tons of bar iron would have paid the debt in 1865—while it would take 35 millions to pay it now, after our twenty years vigorous struggle to reduce it. I cannot quite verify this statement, as I do not know at what time they estimated the debt. However, it is stated in an official price list that cotton averaged about 34.9 cents, in gold, a pound in 1865, and is now about 10½ cents. Bar iron is stated in the same list at $82.40 per ton in gold and is now about $40.00. Roundly speaking, while our debt was one hundred cents in 1865, it is now reduced to fifty-four cents. Then, if one dollar in gold in 1865 would buy no more of any article than fifty-four cents will now, the debt remains unreduced when measured by that particular article.

That very eminent English political economist of the last century, Adam Smith, teaches us that "human labor is a more correct measure of intrinsic value than either gold or silver." But of course, we cannot use human labor as money. I am anxious to see this silver question in the hands of the sovereign people, or as Lincoln used to call us the "common people." It must be taken and decided by us at the ballot box and by our personal influence. Our Congressmen who will be asked to legislate against it are already elected, and our influence, not our votes, is all we have to exercise on the question for the next two years. Let the business man, the farmer, the mechanic, the day laborer ask themselves "can we earn 54 cents to-day as easily as 100 cents in gold in 1865?" To assist in this calculation I might mention that the average premium on gold in 1865 was about 57 per cent. Do not ask only what is the price of articles to-day compared with those in 1865, but ask yourself what are your chances of getting the money itself. It makes but little difference how cheap articles may be, unless you have either credit or cash to buy. Then, if you find that it is just as difficult to get 54 cents to-day, as it was to get a dollar in 1865, then the national debt to you individually has not been reduced as a burden. It is true there are more of us to carry the load, as in 1865 it was estimated at $78.25 for each individual; now it is not more than $26.00. Then the annual interest was about $4.29; now, it is scarcely a dollar for each of us. So we have something to show for our $18,000. hourly payments for twenty years.

Pensions.

There is another well defined and sacred national debt that we must pay, although it is not a bonded debt. The pensions paid to our soldiers and sailors and their dependents amount, roundly, to about 58 million dollars a year for the past five years and may grow rather than decrease. If we take this debt in sums that we can mentally master, it is over $6,600. per hour. We can walk off, as a nation, under all of these burdens with a smile.

But let our people be oppressed by unwise legislation and we will probably see the same disorganization that is seen in Europe. In fact we see ugly signs of these things occasionally now in our strikes and labor troubles. In the long run, this would mean more soldiers, more debts, more pensions, and all the evils that fall on a badly governed nation. I have been trying to get you to grasp the idea that the national debt is a very large element in the discussion of this silver question. The amount, however, is so great that no man can comprehend its magnitude.

Our National Debt as it would appear on Wheels.

Allow me, for your amusement, to mount this debt on wheels and let us have an imaginary parade. If every dollar contained in the National treasury was paid out on June 30, 1885, we can see by the official report that we would have about 1485 million dollars remaining unpaid—as a debt—without even one solitary silver dollar left unused to settle it. Knowing the weight of a gold dollar, you can calculate if you see fit on your thumb nail, that this debt unprovided for, except by the future products of human labor, will weigh over 2443 full legal United States tons of 2240 lbs. avoirdupois. Put this on wheels in ordinary coal carts, each carrying a full ton and give each horse and cart the space of eighteen feet as standing room, and you will have a *golden* procession reaching over eight miles in length. To one familiar with Philadelphia, the picture becomes more graphic, if you will imagine these carts filling up Chestnut Street from curb to curb, four abreast, and the procession extending from the Delaware to the Schuylkill river.

Put it in silver dollars and the weight would be increased sixteen times, and our imaginary parade would extend nearly one hundred and thirty miles. Think of a lumbering train of carts extending from Philadelphia to Washington, loaded with silver dollars measuring our national debt—remaining after the Government vaults might be entirely emptied of what are most uncharitably called the *useless* silver dollars! If the people can obtain, by any such graphic methods as I have seen fit to use, a clearer idea of the national debt, and then multiply that sum, as great as it is, by five or six, they will approximate to the total debts of the community, as estimated by some very reliable statistician. Then keep it before your mind all the time, that the intrinsic value of the full legal tender coined money of a nation is the measure of the value of all of these debts made payable in legal money. Every silver dollar that is coined has a constant tendency to decrease the demand and importance, and hence the bullion or intrinsic value of the gold dollar, and thus justly lighten the burden of debt. Hence, we say with great earnestness, let the good work of coining these dollars go on to the full capacity of our mints. These debts are our debts, made under our own laws; the remainder of the civilized world are spectators, but they can not make laws for us, nor can we make laws for them. Monetary laws of different Governments may produce the most marked effects on other nations, but there are some things in which we must and can act independently of the rest of the world. Our nation is not entirely governed by men, who, before they buy a suit of clothes, a carriage, or a set of harness, anxiously inquire if they are in correct English style. Fashion affects us all to a certain extent, but there is a robust, hardy spirit of Americanism that still feels the blood of 1776 running in our veins, and knows that we are old enough and wise enough to settle many of the great problems of political economy on an American basis.

Professor Sumner as an Anti-Silver Advocate.

Professor William G. Sumner, of Yale College, in an elaborate article against the silver coinage in the *Princeton Review* of Nov., 1879, tells his readers that this notion that legislation affects values is "the root error of a dozen mischievous fallacies." Now, this is a simple assertion, on which he builds his arguments, that can be refuted by every thinking man in the country. Coined money is one of the useful tools of trade, which is wisely manufactured by a Government monopoly, in our mints. As silver is one of the metals extensively used, cannot a plain thinking man,—although he may not be in receipt of a handsome salary as a professor of political economy in a first-class college,—see that if national legislation makes a constant demand for the commodity, silver, this demand will have a tendency to increase its bullion value? The want of a legislative demand for silver throughout the commercial world since 1873, is unquestionably one of the positive causes, and in fact, the leading cause, for the decline in the price of silver as bullion. The world's annual supply of silver has increased *very slightly* since 1873. When we compare the world's annual production of silver since 1873, with the amount held by the world previous to this date, the percentage is seen to be very trifling.

In running the mint establishments, there is a constant demand for machinery, coal, wood, acids, copper, zinc, tin, and a thousand different articles needed in an ordinary manufactory. Each article used has a tendency to increase the demand and hence the price. But when the articles in demand are like gold and silver, of which the world's supply is comparatively limited, then the demand is more sharply felt.

In the mass of valuable statistics collected and published by the International Monetary Conference held at Paris in 1881, is a statement that all the gold in use in any way by man would weigh about 30 million troy pounds, and the silver would weigh about 480 millions. They caution us to accept such statistics with some reserve, but we can certainly give them credit for giving us a fair guess, and this is about all this estimate really amounts to. If we accept these data as correct, then the entire pure gold in the world could be cast in a cubical block about twenty-nine feet square; and about twenty-seven of these blocks would represent the silver in bulk. It would make over 11,000 United States tons of gold, of 2240 lbs. avoirdupois, and over 176,000 tons of silver. These are no small quantities, but we must remember that in the human family of over fourteen hundred million, the share of each would be small. Without depending too much on such statistics, we all know that both gold and silver are comparatively scarce commodities. This scarcity is a very important element in establishing the value of these precious metals. Many are not aware that an avoirdupois pound of pure gold is valued at 301.46\frac{494}{1186}$, or that it is about forty thousand times more valuable than pig iron; while silver, as bullion, is worth over twenty-one hundred times more than pig iron.

The average price of pure silver for the fiscal year, ending June 30, 1884, is given by Mr. Burchard, the late director of the United States Mint, in his official annual report, at 1.11\frac{88}{100}$ per ounce. This would make the silver dollar worth over 86¼ cents. In July, 1876, our silver dollar was worth only 79¼ cents. Silver is worth, at present prices, about one hundred and forty-eight times as much as copper. In old historic times, and even up to the commencement of this century, copper played a minor part as one of the money metals. The people of the world were poorer, and copper was much dearer than now. On account of the great abundance and decreased value of copper, as well as its marked unfitness for a money metal, when compared to either gold or silver, the civilized world has wisely discarded it entirely, except as a minor coin metal. The debts of the world have not been made on a copper basis, while they have been made on a gold and silver basis. This makes a great distinction. There are said to be at least nineteen other metals worth from one thousand to ten thousand dollars an avoirdupois pound, but none of them are fit for money metals. As silver bullion is now worth about one hundred and forty-eight times more than copper, and gold nearly twenty-nine hundred times, this should show that the united wisdom of the world has been indorsed when they used copper but moderately, and have now abandoned it as a full legal tender money metal. The weight of copper produced by one Michigan mining company exceeds all the silver of the world.

Congress has put a forced Legal Valuation on Gold.

It is somewhat remarkable that gold is the only commodity in use in the United States that Congress, by a positive law, has fixed a price for, and offers to buy all that is presented for sale to them. This price is 20.67\frac{74}{87}$ per Troy ounce. You might carelessly look at the laws and not observe the fact. By the law of Jan. 14, 1875, all charge for converting gold bullion of the United States standard into coin, was removed, and all gold offered, must be coined by order of a former law. Hence, gold is the metal that is particularly favored, and has a *forced valuation* given to it by legislation. England and Germany have similar laws, giving gold a fixed, and at the same time a forced, bullion value. This we believe to be a grave economic mistake. The silver producer must take his chances of selling his production at market rates. But the price of gold is fixed by the government simply because the legislative demand says so, and not on account of any of its really superior qualities. To convert a commodity such as bullion gold, although it might be brought to our mints of exactly the right standard of 900 fine for coinage, costs perhaps one per cent. of its value. If this is a fair estimate, and if it costs ten cents to coin a ten dollar gold-piece, then the government has paid ten cents above the market price for that bullion. One per cent. on the nearly six hundred million dollars' worth of gold bought by the government since this law went into effect, makes a direct bounty or *subsidy* paid to those who furnished the government with gold. This bounty or subsidy would amount to perhaps five million dollars.

Our golden coins are beautiful and accurate specimens of mechanical work, and before bullion can be converted into coin, some one must pay for the services of the skilled workman, and defray the natural waste and expense of materials. Our coinage laws should be changed, and *every* material used by these government manufacturing monopolies called mints, should be purchased fairly in the open market, at the market price.

The expense of coinage, as it is for the benefit of the people, is always legitimate for the government. Mints are under the charge of Congress, and as the appropriations for carrying on the mints are made by them, they certainly should have the capacity to decide from year to year, the kind and number of the coin required, and make complete provision for their manufacture. We may not always approve of the decisions of Congress, and some people would be glad to relieve them from all legislation and make all the national laws themselves—*but that is not the American way.* Congress represents the people, and if we do not like their style of doing business, it is our privilege and duty to select wiser and better men. We, the people, are to blame for a shameful neglect among ourselves for not being better informed on more of the commanding issues of the day, and then selecting representatives who are both able and willing to represent us properly. For instance, I have met hundreds of intelligent people who have no more knowledge of this silver question, than they have of the articles of furniture in the Pope's bedroom at Rome. They would perhaps read a description of this furniture with more interest than anything bearing on a question they consider so dry and uninteresting as this one. Yet, some of these very people would work most patiently and laboriously over their desk, counter, or work bench, at the forge or in the field, for ten or twelve hours a day, and not realize that the proper decision of this question, has a most important bearing in measuring the *value* of every stroke of work done by them throughout the weary day.

An Editor's Mistake.

A few years ago, the editor of one of the leading daily newspapers of Philadelphia said to me, when

I was remonstrating with him on his opposition to the silver coinage, that his principal reason against the coinage was because the government had acted so dishonestly in reducing its weight. He would not lend his support to such an outrage! Five minutes devoted to the study of the question by this professed leader of men's thoughts, would have cleared his mind of this often repeated delusion. This gentleman has changed his business.

American Bankers' Association, 1884.

In August, 1884, at the convention of the American Bankers' Association at Saratoga, a polished scholarly gentleman, of spotless reputation, standing deservedly high among the bankers and other citizens of Philadelphia, in a lively speech against the silver dollar coinage, referred to the rascally coin clippers of Great Britain of two centuries ago. Then this crime was regarded as high treason, and punishable with death. He made a comparison between these coin clippers and the congressional majority who passed the act remonetizing the silver dollar in 1878. He said that " the first, clipped the coin after it was made, while Congress directed it to be clipped before it was made." Think of a libel like this uttered by a gentleman on one of the most justifiable acts ever performed by Congress! This speech, in part or in full, was printed and circulated by hundreds of thousands. It may look like presumption, to accuse this gentleman of want of examination of the case, as the study of money is his special business, his life-long profession—but is he not sadly mistaken?

The Panic of 1873-79.

A great many of our people struck snags in the panic of 1873 to 1879, that we have since found out were ignorantly planted there by financiers as eminent as the Hon. John Sherman. Events have taught me facts that argument could not teach, and ever since then I have been looking for more snags, planted by men who have a reputation for financial wisdom. Knowing that a large number of my fellow-citizens—the common people—who do the fighting and the voting of the nation, did not have the same opportunity as myself to hunt up some of these hidden snags, has given me the confidence to offer my services as a volunteer pilot. Arguments do not count in many cases. Prejudice is stronger than argument. Mathematicians do not waste time in arguments on mathematical points. They give facts and make demonstrations and that settles matters. No amount of argument that any one could give would weigh a grain in influencing the judgment of some men. In this plea for fair play all I ask of you is to try and find out if my facts are reliable. If you see fit throw my supposed arguments to one side but do not neglect the facts. I have tried to give the history of the silver dollar correctly. Have you not been deceived again and again when you have been told that it is a clipped, a light weight, a dishonest coin?

Perhaps we have not given this last and vital point

sufficient attention. If the silver dollar is not an honest coin, then our mints should be closed to their coinage, and the mouths of its friends closed to its further defence.

In an open letter published in the *Century Magazine*, February, 1884, I endeavored to show that this coinage was both honest and expedient. The letter was not answered because, I suppose, it was unanswerable, but it was gaily commented upon by that versatile economic scholar, Mr. Horace White, who utterly failed to see the points that I had convinced myself would be perfectly clear to minds much less brilliant than his. What must be done in like cases, except to give up the struggle with such men? He was unable to see the facts as I had presented them, and as he was unable to contradict any one of them, the question had to be left to a discerning public, who might take the trouble to read our diverse views on this subject with clearer brains.

The Silver Dollar always contains 100 cents.

A gentleman of high standing in Philadelphia, whose income is rumored to be about one thousand dollars a day, once said to me, that he would be perfectly satisfied with the silver dollar coinage if the government would put *a hundred cents*'·worth of silver in each one. We have shown that the quantity of pure silver has never been reduced from the first coinage, and the only debasement of the silver dollar is the removal in 1837 of one pound of copper out of the coinage of two thousand dollars. We have also shown that there was about 6¼ per cent. of gold taken from the gold dollar in 1834, or in this case $133.50 less gold was taken to coin two thousand dollars. Here was a heavy debasement, but it was Constitutional, and under the circumstances perhaps was proper.

This was done to keep our coin of gold and silver in circulation concurrently. It was a partial failure. We are doing better now, and we see these coins of the two metals circulating concurrently, although their relative bullion value differs so widely. Our present coinage laws are much wiser than the old ones were.

What was said could not be done, is done. Gold and silver coins of unequal intrinsic value are circulated concurrently. We are not losing our gold, and although there are many fears and predictions on the subject, we will not lose it on account of the silver dollar coinage, for the next quarter of a century. I do not state this as a fact, but only make a little effort at prophesying. We can easily lose our gold from other causes. We have lost it before and can again, but not if we exercise, as a nation, the commonest kind of common sense.

We have made this little digression before we have tried to answer the one thousand dollar a day gentleman concerning the neglect of the government, doing like the bread bakers, making a fresh batch of dollars each day, expressly to use on that day. If we should, then we think perfect satisfaction could be given to all. Of course our very intelligent friend did not mean that, but only wished the government to be liberal and add 15 or 18 per cent. more silver to the dollar, and happiness would reign.

That brilliant and clear-headed statesman, Alexander Hamilton, who was the Secretary of the Treasury under Washington, in a report on the establishment of the mint in 1791, observed in regard to the word "*cent*";—" that being in use in various transactions and instruments, will, without much difficulty, be understood as the *hundredth*." In fact, the United States had already coined copper cents by private contract. It is the simple abbreviation of the Latin word "*centum*" or one hundred. We adopted the new word as meaning the one hundredth part of our dollars. The silver dollar itself was a coin very extensively in use for almost three centuries before this time, deriving its Austrian name, "*thaler*," from the "*thal*" or valley in which it was coined. At the time we organized our mint, under the fostering care of this eminent financier, we also adopted this old and well-known word " dollar " as the name of our money of account, the word cents or hundredths being expressly named in our law, as one of the fractional names of our money of account. It is just as the English name their " pounds," the French their " francs " and the Germans their " marks " and fractions thereof. Provision in this law was made for coining dollars out of the two metals gold and silver. We did not coin single dollar pieces out of gold until 1849, but the larger gold coins were made. Each kind of money was exactly on a par, or in the words of the law was: " a lawful tender in all payments whatsoever." This was done in obedience to the sentiments of Hamilton in the report I have referred to as he said: " that it seemed to him most advisable not to attach the unit exclusively to either one of the metals because this cannot be done effectually without destroying the office and character of one of them as money, and reducing it to the situation of mere merchandise." Washington and Jefferson, as well as the custom and public sentiment of the times, backed up this opinion. These old gentlemen were not experts in electricity, and steam and other nineteenth century knowledge, but we have only to read some of their productions to become profoundly impressed with their wisdom on the money question. They had just passed through with the Continental paper currency troubles of our revolutionary days of 1776, and their instincts were keen and bright from friction. They perhaps remembered that at one time during the revolutionary war, the full legal currency of the country had so far depreciated that a barrel of flour was worth $1,576. and John Adams paid $15,000. for a suit of clothes and a hat. Many of the facts I have laid before you are buried in old laws and dry official documents. Every intelligent man should study this question, to a certain extent, for himself. Coining money is an act of sovereignty, and we, the people, are the kings and rulers in this democratic land and should be able to decide intelligently on the subject.

When this thousand dollar a day gentleman said that he wanted the silver dollar to contain one hundred cents, he said what you may hear every day—from men who do not clear one dollar a day. He looked at gold as the fixed, unvarying centre of intrinsic value around which silver as well as every other species of property continually revolved. There is another representative philosopher in another branch of science. The Rev. John Jasper of Richmond, Va., who teaches his flock that the earth is the fixed centre of the universe, and in his classic way tells them, "the sun do move." Now this doctrine taught by Jasper, in the science of astronomy, is not more utterly absurd nor more universally condemned than this notion in the science of finance, that the intrinsic value of gold is fixed in the markets of the world. Now how to get at either one of these representative philosophers, I am at a perfect loss, unless they are willing to study the respective questions, concerning which they have received such false notions. But study will not reach some men. An event, like the loss of all property and income, has a wonderful tendency to brighten up a man's wits on money matters. I feel inclined to think that if I had an income of a thousand dollars a day, for the last nine years, I would know less about the silver question and more about what was necessary to fit up a handsome city and country residence or a first-class steam yacht.

Be assured, that there are one hundred cents in silver in each silver dollar, and only one hundred cents' worth of gold in each gold dollar. Although the silver hundredth or cent is not worth quite as much as the gold hundredth or cent, it is not the fault of the Government. There is no dishonesty about it. The Government might, constitutionally, reduce the weight of the gold dollar and make its bullion value equal to the silver dollar. We most emphatically say, leave each dollar untampered with, and in all probability should either Germany or England re-establish practical bi-metallism as they probably will, and as we have in the United States—silver would reach its old position. We are watching and waiting and see signs, but signs only so far. In the mean time stand by the debt contracts and make no change in the weight or fineness of our full legal tender money. Who can say that it is not the gold dollar that has become dearer, and not the silver dollar that has become cheaper? During the last few years have not prices fallen in a greater ratio than is now existing between the value of the bullion in these respective dollars? As we have seen in regard to the price of cotton and bar iron for the last twenty years, we may also see that reliable economists say that the average fall of prices during the past three years has been about 20 per cent. This will more than cover the difference between the present price of the gold and the silver bullion in the respective dollars.

The Unit.

Several specimen old silver dollars of 1795-99 and 1802 are now on my table, and have stamped, in depressed letters, on the edge of the coin, "one dollar or unit... hundred cents." This word "unit" of course means that this is "one" of the measures in which we kept our accounts. We coined half units, in the fifty-cent pieces and quarters, tenths and twentieths all of silver. The gold was coined in "ten dollars or units" expressly so specified in the law and called an eagle. Half and quarter eagles were provided for also in the law of 1792. These being the two coined dollars, the one, the silver being coined in one single piece or unit and the gold eagle being coined in the shape of ten units. Let it be most distinctly remembered that the full legal tender coins of the United States were made of both metals and their value was based on both metals. We were a double standard or bi-metallic nation from the organization of our mints until 1873. In 1806 we coined no dollars in silver but full legal tender coins were coined regularly until 1853. During this time, foreign silver dollars were a legal tender at a value fixed by the Government, and extensively used. Up to 1853, we coined about 87 millions of silver and about 326 millions of gold. In 1836, but 1000 silver dollars were coined; then in 1839 the coinage of the silver dollar was again resumed, and it was coined regularly every year after that (except in 1858), up to 1873. In fact, in 1872 and 1873, we coined over two million silver dollars. We admit that the total coinage of silver was comparatively small. The *only year* previous to 1873, when we did not coin some full legal tender coins of silver was in 1858. The total gold coinage of our mints amounts in round numbers up to 1873, to about 817 million, and about 92 millions of the silver coinage up to that date was "a lawful tender in all payments whatsoever." Now how absurd, how unfair for the advocates of the gold standard to tell the people that the word "coin" so distinctly defined as a legal tender in all of our laws up to 1873 does not mean anything but gold coin! The 3¾ per cent. higher bullion value of the silver dollar over gold during our war years was the *sole* cause of so little silver being coined during those years. For years the heavy coin payments of the Government were made in the 96 or 97 cent gold dollars, measured by silver. That is the Government wisely took the option that our double legal standard gave them and paid their coin debts *in these cheaper gold dollars*. This was not only, the value of these dollars at home, but it was their value in London, then as now, the great commercial and financial centre of the world. If a merchant wanted silver to take to London or Paris to settle balances, he had to pay a premium on it. So the reason that we did not use silver dollars to pay our coin debts during our greenback days was *not* because the Government could not get silver for coinage—it was *not* because our creditors would not have been pleased to receive it, but it was *solely* because the gold was the cheaper dollar.

Custom duties payable in coin.

Our import custom duties during these days were made payable in coin, not gold coin, not silver coin, but the word of the law is simply, "*coin*." Our merchants could have bought silver in the markets of the world and our mints were always open to the coinage of full legal tender silver dollars. But the importing merchants, finding that the Government was true to its laws and demanded only coin for customs, they, in turn, obtained the cheaper coin, gold, and settled their custom dues. It was all perfectly fair and honorable and is a part of the bimetallic system. Facts like these are continually forgotten, suppressed, or denied. Newspapers of the highest repute in financial matters are continually making this mistake in saying our duties were payable in gold only.

The demonetization of silver in 1873-74, a huge blunder.

Mr. Hooper, who had charge of the bill stopping the coinage of the silver dollar, in the House of Representatives, in 1873, in his speech on the subject, gave as one of the reasons for this stoppage, that as the Government could get the gold to make a gold dollar more than three per cent. cheaper than they could get silver to make a silver dollar, and as we had exceedingly heavy coin obligations to meet, it was wise to provide for the coinage of gold alone. This was about as wise as to cut off the left hand, because the right hand was temporarily able to do the best work. But, wonderful to say, both Congress and the people at that time entirely failed to see the inconsistency of the reasoning. The mass of the people had nearly forgotten all about gold and silver money, as it was distinctly an age of paper money. As our Government was under the double standard law, from 1792 to 1873, then we became for five years and two months a single standard country. This new law distinctly stated that the gold dollar should, "*be the unit of value.*" This was perfectly consistent as we had abandoned our well tried double standard to specify what should be our single standard. If it was not part of the constitutional power of Congress to regulate the value of our coins, then all legal debts made by the Government under this single standard law—there might be an equitable, but no legal claim—for the payment of all such debts in gold alone. But ever since that time, and particularly now, when we are so well prepared to pay some coin obligations in silver alone, there is no one who holds a coin obligation of the United States who cannot sell that obligation for gold. All the bonds will sell even at a premium in gold and some of them at a premium of 26 per cent.

The effect of the law of 1873, on the unit of value.

The term "unit of value," used in our laws, does not, obviously, mean that Congress could fix the purchasing value of the coin—or what is the same thing fix prices—but refers exclusively and distinctly to its debt-paying value only. This is not made distinct by the words alone—yet its meaning is apparent. Hence, when in the law of 1878, Congress restored the debt-paying value to the silver dollar, although, that clause of the law, of 1873, making gold the unit of value was not rescinded—it was virtually and most directly annulled. Hence we have now, as we had by the law of 1792, two well defined units of value, the gold and the silver dollar, either one of which is declared by law to be a full legal tender for all payments, unless otherwise expressly stipulated in the contract.

The clipped gold dollar.

It is a little singular that although, from 1834 to 1873, the bullion value of the silver dollar exceeded the bullion value of the gold dollar from one to six per cent., that we never heard of any complaint against the dishonest, the clipped, the light weight gold dollar. This mono-metallic craze, did not get a fair start in the world until about 1873. It was so local in England and in a few other countries that the world was not distressed over it; but when two countries like Germany and the United States caught the economic disease, becoming gold mono-metallic, then the entire commercial world commenced to feel the pangs. We, alone, cannot cure the world of this distress. Events, not arguments, will be the only sure cure. But events do not always educate, although, they far excel arguments as a school teacher.

The Philadelphia Press.

It was refreshing to read this brief editorial article in the Philadelphia *Press* of December 17, 1883.

For reasons entirely satisfactory to its management, this paper has been particularly earnest in denouncing the silver coinage. But please read the article in full. "Silver coinage is suggesting all sort of devices to check its evils, but the way and only way to stop the harm of silver coinage is to stop the coinage. Five years ago the silver bill was passed amid the shrieking predictions that it meant ruin. *It has not.* If silver coinage is stopped now our currency will remain reasonably sound, a composite fabric of gold, silver and paper framed by the *logic of events* always and everywhere wiser than the reasonings of men."

Now here is a frank confession that somebody made a mistake in shrieking predictions of ruin in 1878, but just here this editor takes a fresh breath and shrieks again, that the harm predicted was yet to come. Since then, we have added about 50 millions to our stock of silver dollars and ruin from this cause has not yet overtaken us, but this newspaper still shrieks. Events had educated that writer, when arguments failed. On February 19, 1885—this same excellent newspaper, forgetting, for the time, all about the energetic fight it had been making for a higher tariff and Republican success at the late Presidential election, attributed the depressed condition of business to this continued silver coinage. If this is the true cause of the present " hard times " then the shrieking predictions of 1878 have been realized. We believe that without this coinage of silver by our country, the " hard times " would be far more severe. Our troubles arise *in spite of this coinage* which has a constant tendency to relieve us of some of our burdens. This is the question that we, the people, must try and master. Is our silver coinage a wise or unwise measure? is the problem we must solve.

Ernest Seyd and Hon. Wm. D. Kelley.

Let us turn to the words of wisdom uttered by the late Mr. Ernest Seyd, one of the most able and reliable statisticians and financiers of Great Britain. He was the author of a very able and exhaustive book, advocating the restoration of the double standard to Great Britain, and his efforts are said to have produced a profound impression on his conservative countrymen. But financial disasters or events have done more in this direction than the able arguments of Mr. Seyd. In 1867, this far-sighted and clear-headed financier, in discussing this question, that was then exciting considerable interest, expressed himself very freely on the evils that would probably fall on the world, in an attempt to discard silver as a full legal tender money metal. He said that "throughout the world a fall in prices would take place, injurious alike to the owners of solid property and to the laboring classes, and advantageous only, and unjustifiably so, to the holders of state debts and other contracts of that kind." He also said, that when these results followed the discarding of silver, all sorts of reasons would be brought forward to account for the distress, and thus the real cause would be neglected until this distress compelled thinking men to refer it to the legitimate cause.

These views of this clear-headed thinker were considered of such importance, that the Hon. Wm. D. Kelley, of the House of Representatives, in a speech of May 18, 1878, submitted an article on this subject by Mr. Seyd, and it was published in full as part of the *Congressional Record.*

At that time Judge Kelley was an ardent friend of the silver dollar coinage. He still calls himself a bi-metallist, but, unfortunately for bi-metallism, his influence is thrown against the further coinage of the silver dollar in our country for the present. He has introduced a bill in Congress to virtually stop this silver coinage. In a series of most charming letters written from Europe, in the summer of 1879 for the Philadelphia *Times*, and reprinted in pamphlet form by Messrs. Porter & Coates, of Philadelphia, he gives the opinion that the gold dollar should be increased in weight, or that the silver dollar should be reduced so as to make our ratio of the use of these metals more nearly conform to the general European ratio of 15½ of silver to 1 of gold. That is, he proposes to add about 3 cents' worth of gold to the gold dollar, or take away about 3 cents' worth of silver from the silver coin. We admit that there would be some advantages in either plan, but we condemn both plans as impracticable and unwise. He remarks incidentally, that he who will suggest any other method than either of these plans, by which we can establish bi-metallism on a basis that other nations can accept, will entitle himself to eternal fame. As Judge Kelley is one of my neighbors, and is the gentleman who represents me personally in Congress,

I am thus particular in stating his position. When he had the privilege of voting for the remonetization of silver, in 1878, he did his part in winning for himself a share of this eternal fame that he so generously offers to others. When his vote assisted to swell the handsome number of 189 to 79 in the House of Representatives, against the veto of the silver bill by President Hayes, he obtained another generous slice of eternal fame. This vote over the veto, prevented the President from perpetuating one of the most enormous economic crimes against the people. This vote enables them to have a chance, at least, to pay the national debt according to the contract. Perhaps the dishonor of this veto, in the eyes of the future historians of our country, will far exceed the honor of having been President of the United States for four years. I would not exchange this dishonor for all the honor and emoluments of the Presidency. It was a gigantic attempt to steal the products of millions of days' labor from our people, that were never pledged to be paid. Let us have the charity to believe that it was a mistake in motive or judgment; but in effect, would it not have been an enormous crime?

The bi-metallism re-established in our country in 1878, is doing its work about as far as our country alone can do to regulate the monetary affairs of the world. We regret that the execution of the law has been in the hands of an executive administration always bitterly hostile to the law, and that the minimum amount allowed (that is two million dollars' worth of silver per month) has always been chosen instead of the maximum amount,—four millions. Remember that this silver bullion is bought at market rates, but the money paid for it is not necessarily gold, but it can be paid for in greenbacks or silver dollars. Buying silver need not diminish the amount of gold held by the government.

International Money and Forced Valuation.

If we can secure, by an international treaty, or by an informal agreement, or by our example, the full coöperation of the leading nations of the world, to do just as we are doing,—go ahead and coin full legal tender coins out of both metals—then practical bi-metallism throughout the world would be secured. The important change should be made in the general coinage laws of the world, so that each government should *buy* all the materials necessary for coinage at the market price, and directly regulate the kind and number of coins made. No nation should put a forced valuation on either metal as is now done on gold by the United States, Germany, and Great Britain. We think that this *forced* legal valuation of gold bullion will be found to be a serious economic mistake, that will be corrected in the future. Think of the effect of this law, now favoring the gold producers, when compared with the present law—so slightly favoring the silver producers!

It would be exceedingly beneficial if we could all agree on one precise ratio as to the use of silver and gold in coinage, and have the same proportion of alloy, and even give our coin the same general appearance and dimensions. The unification of all the full legal tender coins in the world, or international money made of both metals, would be an extraordinary stroke of good luck and wisdom. It has been well worthy of the ambition of the most able of men to reach for this; but at present an innocent child might as well beg its indulgent mother to hang the moon on its little crib. A common language, a common system of weights and measures, are even more desirable revolutions. But must we stop writing and speaking until we get this common language? Must we stop weighing and measuring commodities until we can adopt this much desired, universally accepted, system of weights and measures? We fear that neither one of these three tremendously progressive reforms is at all probable in our day and generation. We must worry along in our old and badly fitting suit of clothing.

Some people seem to forget that we have a large family of about 57 millions of the most active people in the world, to look after, under our own flag. It is for ourselves that we demand legislation from Congress. It is for ourselves that the silver dollar is being coined. Our domestic trade and domestic debts exceed, in a wonderful proportion, all our foreign trade and debts. I would not advocate the coinage of a single dollar expressly for exportation, neither of silver or of gold. Adverse balances of trade can usually be adjusted by stamped bullion, gold or silver, about as easily as in coin. Such stamped bars are now legally furnished to merchants by the government and are extensively used. First-class governments care nothing for our coin, it is only the bullion in the coin that is wanted. Our money is no longer money when it gets from under our flag. Considerable experience in foreign travel for years, has taught me that our beautiful gold or silver coined money is received by the bulk of foreigners one comes in contact with, very much as they receive one's requests, spoken, perhaps, in good, round English tones. If you want to buy to advantage, you must exchange your money for theirs; and if you wish to speak, so as to be understood, you must use their language.

Foreign Money not Money with us—but only Metal.

In the fiscal year ending June 30, 1881, it is reported that we threw more than one hundred million dollars' worth of foreign gold coin into the melting pots of the U. S. Assay Office at New York City. We converted their beautiful coins into bullion, at a waste of material and workmanship of perhaps one million dollars. When our nation has nothing else to settle balances with, excepting the coin, of course then the coin must go,—but when not under our flag it is *metal*, not money.

Our Silver Coinage need not drive our Gold Coins out of Circulation.

One constant complaint, from gentlemen of the highest financial standing is that this silver coinage will drive gold to a premium or out of circulation, and at last out of the country. This is a serious charge and should be looked into very closely. First, let me observe, that France has been under this bi-metallic system for nearly a century, and it is reported officially that she has over 537 million dollars' worth of full legal tender silver coin in circulation, and 848 million dollars' worth of gold. The paper money is 548 million. So you see that taking the number of her people in consideration, she has almost as much paper money per head as we have, and as to gold and silver, she excels us by a large sum. This is an event that should educate,—but our gold men will not or can not see it. England has only about 589 millions of gold—while Germany has only about 335—but France has almost as much as both of these countries.

Now let us look into our home affairs and study the question as it appears here. The amount of gold estimated to be in our country on June 30, 1878, before the silver coinage made any impression, was 244 million dollars. This estimate is given in the annual report of the late Dr. Linderman, who was then the Director of the United States Mint. Now let us see what his successor, the Hon. H. C. Burchard, the late Director of the U. S Mint, says in his annual report for June, 1884. He estimates the gold in the United States to be 610 million dollars. Here we see an increase of 366 million dollars in gold during the first six years of our silver dollar coinage. The next annual report, will doubtless show a very handsome addition to this sum. If we lose our gold during the next twenty years of silver coinage, at the present slow rate of coinage it will be from other causes. I can see no possible reason why any one should pay a premium for gold coin, unless the national administration should see fit to annul the laws made by Congress and refuse to recognize the silver dollar as a legal coin. When clearly defined laws made by Congress are repudiated by our executive officers, we are prepared for trouble, and public sentiment should be awakened. The law should be supreme.

Our Gold increasing—Not decreasing.

In regard to the country losing her gold, we have some facts bearing on the case that will illustrate very plainly that we can lose it without an excess of silver coinage. In 1847, the year before we discovered gold in California, it was estimated that we had about 120 million dollars in gold and silver specie in the United States; we have shown that we did not coin a great deal of silver from 1847 to 1860, as it was the dearer metal, yet our specie was increased in those thirteen years. How much, you may breathlessly inquire? Well—it was estimated that we had 257 million of specie in 1860, thus in thirteen years, we had increased our specie fund 137 million dollars. This, remember, was both gold and silver. Compare this with the 366 millions of an increase of gold alone under our six years of silver coinage. Here is a statement that should startle us: during the thirteen fiscal years from June 30, 1848, to June

30, 1861, it is officially stated, that the United States production of gold reached the immense sum of over 1836 million dollars.

We do not ask you to put too much confidence in these official estimates, as they do not pretend to be more than a close approximate guess. It seems to be impossible to obtain such statistics accurately. They are the estimates made by those who are employed by the Government to obtain all of the reliable data possible. Without statistics we know that we were not flush with specie in our country at any time from 1848 to 1861, and we also know that enormous quantities of gold were produced in California. It is evident, then, that we lost nearly all of our California gold—sending it adrift in the world. Our gold fields are now, apparently, greatly exhausted. Now, we are adding to our gold fund—then, we were losing it. You can see then, that a nation can get rid of its gold without excessive silver coinage. Adopt the same kind of national housekeeping that we had from 1848 to 1861, and we can lose the most of our gold as well as our silver. As we once found out exactly how to do it, we have confidence in the wisdom of our people that one lesson of that kind is sufficient to educate us not to do it again. While we were so lavishly pouring our stream of gold into the markets of the world, Australia was doing about as well on the opposite side of the earth. The industries and commerce of the world were wonderfully stimulated during those years.

The World's Production of the Precious Metals.

It has been estimated by eminent statisticians, that if we would add together the sum of gold in use in the world when Columbus discovered America—(1492), to that produced up to 1850,—that the amount produced since 1850 would be about equal to the other sum; while the amount of silver produced in the world since 1850, will not equal the one-third of the sum estimated to have been in use when Columbus discovered America and that produced up to 1850. Hence, you may observe that the silver production during the past thirty-five years has not been very remarkable when compared with the production of gold. We should keenly remember that the business necessities of the world for the money metals have increased at a wonderful rate in the past thirty-five years. This excessive gold production since 1850, is what gave the leaders of the gold mono-metallic party the idea that coined money was going to become too cheap, and that the legal debts of the world were in a fair way to be wiped out at half their value. This reason is frankly given by some of the most prominent European mono-metallists. That reason is most carefully and wisely suppressed by the mono-metallists before the American people. The world's annual production of gold has been gradually *decreasing*. The California production reached its height in 1853 and Australia's in 1856. Steam, electricity, and many other scientific achievements have stimulated the industrial and commercial activities of the world to a phenomenal rate of progress. We need a larger and larger supply of real money, and notwithstanding the heavy burdens laid on representative money, such as: paper money, checks, drafts, bills of exchange, telegraphic and post-office orders, and all other varieties, we must stand faithfully by the well-tried, but only universal measures of intrinsic value—gold and silver, as full legal tender money. The gold and silver does the measuring, while the other varieties of money may do 99 per cent. of the other duty. Gold and silver alone are real money—all the rest are simply "evidences of debt." We repeat—we cannot abandon the use of either of these metals, without almost doubling the legal debts of the civilized world, and decreasing by nearly one-half the intrinsic value of all other forms of property—as well as the prices of all the products of human labor and the wages of workingmen. To emphasize this, —we may give the official estimate of the increase in the national debts of Europe from 1865 to 1879. In 1865—the amount was 12,503 million dollars; in 1879 it had increased to 20,585 millions—an increase, as you will see, of over 8000 million dollars. They still increase at a prodigious rate. National debts are rated as one of our modern inventions—blessings in disguise some people foolishly call them.

The amount of Gold and Silver Money in Use.

Mr. Burchard, in his last annual report, estimates that there was about 3294 millions of gold money in use in the world and about 2755 millions of silver.

Roundly speaking, this makes 54 cents in gold to 46 cents in silver. What nonsense it is then, to speak of gold as *the* money of the world as has been done in grave state papers written by gentlemen occupying the hightest official positions in our country! In Europe, almost one-third of all the legal tender coined money in use is silver.

Legal Tenders.

Let us examine what this term we have been using so often means. Is it not a guard or protection given to a debtor by law, so that a creditor cannot take an unfair advantage of him when the debt is to be settled? Then, practically, any kind of property or any legal title to property that a debtor knows a creditor is anxious and willing to take becomes a legal tender. There is no use of a legal tender law if a creditor can demand whatever may suit his own notions, when a debtor presents himself to settle a legal debt. By our laws, either gold or silver dollars or greenbacks are an unlimited legal tender, except when the law makes other provisions. The debtor can, but the creditor cannot, always take his choice, unless the contract or debt specifies some special method of payment. The contract made with our bondholders is most distinctly specified by the laws, to be a coin contract. This is often denied, but we unreservedly appeal to the U. S. laws, and you will see that they are clear and specific on this point. On this fact being proven, I base all of my reliability as a pilot.

The Government may pay a bondholder in any kind of money the bondholder is willing to accept. Gold bullion, stamped bars, gold or silver certificates, greenbacks, national bank notes, checks, drafts may all be used and be acceptable to the bondholder, but all of them could be legally rejected. But he dare not legally reject either gold or silver dollars and appeal to the people or the courts for redress.

Should the Secretary of the Treasury have the word "gold" printed on the bonds of the United States, instead of the word "coin" as the law directs, he, as an executive officer, would be no more justified in the act, than a Commander of one of our war vessels would be, if on his own responsibility he would declare war on Great Britain and bombard one of her ports. Congress makes the laws, the only duty of these gentlemen is to execute them.

When these debts were made, the bonds were bought at about 57 cents on the dollar in gold or 55 cents in silver, but we must pay a coined dollar of the then standard weight and fineness for each. We have already paid out as we have shown about 3000 million dollars in gold on this contract, and we will probably pay over 2000 million more in coin before we get through with it.

These statistics may tire you, but some of them must be mentally mastered if you wish to understand your positive duty as a citizen of your country in this financial emergency. If I have failed to reach your sympathy or comprehension on this national debt question, then my efforts will be lost. If it were not for debts, the coinage question would be greatly simplified. We could commence again as our forefathers did in 1792. We might make our coin conform to the present bullion value, if we chose. I am inclined to think, after the closest study of this question, that we are now about as near right in our coinage as we could get, had we again perfect freedom to make a change. We cannot get rid of the past, but must manfully face our responsibilities.

The use of the two precious metals as full legal tender money has a constant tendency to decrease the bullion value of the dearer one and increase the bullion value of the cheaper one, providing the cheaper one is chosen as it should be by legislative demand for the largest coinage. The world's very extensive and exceptional free use of gold as a money metal, during the phenomenal production of gold by California and Australia, had a constant automatic tendency to decrease the intrinsic value of the then dearer metal, silver, and increase the bullion value of the cheaper metal, gold. While the monetary revolution so successfully but so unfairly started in 1873, has had a constant tendency to increase the bullion value of gold and decrease the bullion value of silver.

To argue that the use of silver, generally, as a full legal money metal during the period when we were making our huge war debt had no tendency in keeping down the intrinsic value of gold is most unreasonable. No responsible political economist will teach such an absurd notion. Under this double standard system the coinage of the dearer metal may be temporarily stopped, and this bullion may remain in the hands of the people uncoined; but it is the reserved force. From 1856 to 1867, there was no full legal tender silver coined in France, but an enormous quantity of the cheaper metal, gold, was coined. This is an event that should educate. This automatic effect of the two metals regulating the bullion value of each must never be lost to sight or called useless. You might as well call that part of an army, kept in reserve by a skilful commander, useless, if an emergency did not arise to call it into action.

During the late rebellion, I served for over three years on one of our steam war vessels. The noble old frigate carried two very heavy sheet-anchors, carefully lashed amidships, and although engaged in action and some exceedingly arduous and risky duty in blockading the hostile ports during some very severe winter gales, I do not now recall the fact of ever seeing those sheet-anchors disturbed from their lashings. Were these sheet-anchors useless? The money metal for which there may be no legislative demand for coinage because it is temporarily the dearer, is the lashed sheet-anchor ready for use in a monetary emergency. He who discards the utility of the unused money metal, simply because it is the dearer, should be instantly dismissed as unworthy of leadership in the science of finance, just as the commanding officer of a man-of-war would be if he would insist on going to sea without a spare anchor. A court-martial would settle the fate of the naval-officer, and the deliberate judgment of Congress and the people will, we hope, test the capacity of our future financial leaders.

While we do not believe the demonetization of our silver in 1873-74 was so much of a crime as it was a mistake, as many of those who voted for the plan afterwards publicly admitted: that, "they did not know that the gun was loaded." The reverberations of this gun were heard and felt throughout the civilized world. Thousands of worthy and innocent families have been socially and financially wrecked by its effects. Many of them who are still living do not know and have not the least suspicion, even at this time, that this was the leading cause of their disasters.

Senator Sherman as a false pilot.

Mr. George M. Weston, in his most instructive and very valuable work on "The Silver Question," published in 1878, by "Homans" of New York City, gives a full and interesting account of the passage of this law demonetizing silver. Neither the President of the United States, who signed the bill, nor the most of those who voted for it, seemed to know what had been done. The startling fact that we had no silver dollar after 1873-74, was not fairly known, either to Congress or the people, until March, 1876. We had plenty of blind men leading the blind in those days. When Secretary Sherman told us in his annual report, as Secretary of the Treasury, on December 3, 1877, that he did not foresee the fall in the bullion price of silver that was caused by this demonetization; he makes a frank confession that the metaphysics of finance was a mystery to him. By late speeches reported to have been made by him on the Pacific coast this spring, and by the interviews as more lately reported in our daily papers, he seems to have learned but little since 1873, notwithstanding his very high reputation as one of our trusted and practical leaders in the science of finance. He seems to be watching gold, like the Rev. Mr. Jasper does the sun, and from their respective practical standpoints —Jasper *knows* that the earth is the fixed centre of the universe and Mr. Sherman *knows* that gold is the fixed centre of intrinsic value. Hence, his constantly reiterated advice; watch the gold dollar and pile silver into the silver dollar until they are intrinsically equal in value and equally *honest*. Neither events nor arguments have opened his eyes to the libels he has uttered against the honesty of the silver dollar. To argue with him I suppose would be as useless as to send a Presbyterian missionary to Constantinople to try to convert the sultan of Turkey. In 1877, I had the misfortune to put implicit confidence in certain public utterances of Mr. Sherman on finance. Acting on his advice, a small investment was made, and I lost about a thousand dollars in less than a year by it. This little event helped to educate me as to the exact soundness of his financial views. I have been a keen student of Mr. Sherman ever since. Beware of his teachings, and as long as he talks of the dishonest silver dollar and keeps his eye fastened on the gold dollar as the unvarying measure or fixed centre of the financial universe, he will remain a blind leader on this question of finance.

Silver Bullion Certificates, based on Gold Valuation.

There has been a constant effort for some years to stop the coinage of the silver dollar, and at the same time, in order to conciliate the silver producers, to order the same amount of silver to be bought monthly as at present. This uncoined silver bullion is proposed to be stored by the government, and silver certificates are to be issued for it, based alone on the *gold* valuation of the silver bullion. If this plan would not affect the price of bullion silver, then the silver producer would be just as well off under the proposed arrangement as under the existing one.

This plan would have a marked and constant tendency to reduce the bullion value of silver, and every ounce of silver thus bought would be that much silver demonetized. Gold would remain as the sole legally recognized money metal, measuring the value of the silver. We would lose all the automatic effects produced by the continued coinage of silver, in raising its value as bullion, and decreasing the bullion value of gold. Silver producers do not ask for a market for their silver,—as a product like theirs is always in demand. What is needed and demanded by the silver producer, is a fair price in this market. But in the discussion of this question, the special needs or demands of silver producers as such, should be entirely ignored. When we compare the value of their annual products with the commodities produced by many other industries, it is quite insignificant. We, the people, have no more necessity for legal tender certificates based on silver at a gold valuation, than we have for legal tender certificates based on real estate, cotton, or bar iron, at a gold valuation. We, the people, do, however, have urgent need of silver dollars to pay off our national and private debts. We do need the continued coinage of this dollar in order to produce the automatic effect in reducing the bullion value of the other unit of value—the gold dollar. We need the continued coinage of silver dollars as an enlarged basis for our vast fund of paper money. The necessities of the people at large, and not those of the silver producer, have made me one of the ardent advocates of the honesty and expediency of this silver coinage. The use of money in our domestic affairs exceeds all our use for it in foreign affairs, in proportion as a man is to a mouse in size. We cannot pay any portion of our national debt legally, with gold bullion, nor even with gold or silver dollar certificates. The entire scheme for the issue of legal tender certificates on silver bullion, based on its gold valuation, will be a thorough delusion for the real friends of silver. Mr. J. W. Sylvester, of the United States Assay Office, at New York City, published a small pamphlet in 1883, advocating this scheme. . In 1884, he issued a second edition, containing the strongest kind of indorsements from many of the leading newspapers and writers who have been advocating gold mono-metallism. This, alone, should be enough to open the eyes of the friends of the silver dollar for the lurking danger. Cannot General Warner and his friends take a hint?

This is a masked battery, fully manned and equipped by the gold men, and if the ruse is successful it will be a complete victory for those who believe in the "one yardstick" theory. To them it does not make a particle of difference, how much this yardstick expands in length. It will be the same yardstick they assure us, but they do not seem to comprehend the bad effects of its use. We, practical bi-metallists, want our measure of intrinsic value to vary as little as possible from year to year, and we believe in the use of the shorter yardstick when we find the other one is getting too long; we believe that this use of the shorter one has a constant tendency to make it increase in length, and at the same time reduces the length of the longer one. We admit that we always must have, from the nature of things, an elastic measure of intrinsic value, but we want this elasticity to be automatically regulated, and to vary as little as possible. The bi-metallic system does this for us with comparative satisfaction.

The Pendulum as a Measure.

Should an unskilful amateur try to make a good pendulum clock, he might look around very carefully, perhaps, to find a material to make a monometallic pendulum rod, so that the variations from heat and moisture would affect it as little as possible.

He would know that a minute fraction of an inch in the variation of the length of his pendulum rod would seriously affect the qualities of his clock as a correct measurer of time. But now let us watch an expert. He knows that there is no material that is not seriously affected by heat or moisture. He at once adopts a sort of bi-metallism, and will take two metal rods, perhaps of brass and iron, and knows exactly the different ratios in which they will be affected by heat. These two rods will be so arranged by him, in position and in length, that while the heat may expand the one metal so as to lengthen the pendulum rod, it will expand the other metal so as to shorten the rod. The exact length desired will be maintained, and he will show us one of the most accurate of all measures, a scientific clock. If you have forgotten how the common gridiron or compensating pendulum rod is made, we beg of you, at once to refer to some elementary book on the subject, and study the cunning secret, as it so fully illustrates the automatic effect of the use of both silver and gold, in regulating the intrinsic value of the coined money. The supply and demand of the two metals is represented by the heat, while the knowledge of finance, by the skilful law-maker, is represented by the skill of the expert clockmaker.

Here we have a specimen of a fixed measure of length, but we most distinctly declare that no kind of money is a fixed measure of intrinsic value. All that we insist upon, is that by the judicious use of both gold and silver as full legal tender money, we obtain *a far more steady measure of intrinsic value* than we could by the use of either one alone. This idea, the common sense and practice of the world has indorsed for many centuries, and is universally commended by scientific financiers. This disposition is even shown by some mono-metallists, who say they do not want to discard the use of silver; in fact, they are even more anxious than we silver dollar men are, to use more silver. They want to make the silver dollar at least 15 per cent. larger. We practical bi-metallists want to use our silver with gold, to make the pendulum rod of our clock or measure—these others do not see this point exactly—but are willing to make the entire clock case of silver, without legislation, but the pendulum rod that measures, must be made of gold alone.

Is it not time that the theory of these gold revolutionists of 1873, should be abandoned? These people are telling us to stick to one yardstick, perfectly regardless of the evident truth, that this golden yardstick may be made to almost double its length by carrying out their plans in full. We may have the same gold dollar, but it might take twice as many days' labor or twice the product of labor in all other pursuits, except in gold mining, to get that dollar, caused by this special legislative demand for gold. In other words, all the legal debts might remain the same in dollars or measured by this golden yardstick, but measured by ordinary human labor the debts might be doubled. Is this fair, is this honest when we bear in mind that we had the two measures or the compensating measure in use, when the debts were contracted? Is not this question put in such a way that a man of common education and judgment can answer it just as well as a political economist? If you have failed to grasp this pendulum rod illustration in the one reading—please let me advise you to look over it the second time. There are men with such peculiar minds that no one could make the simple gridiron pendulum expedient clear, but I hope none of these are wasting time over a book like this.

Political economy has a bad flavor to many people, as they can truly say the leaders differ so widely in their teachings. But remember, this is only an effort to learn how a nation may live well and wisely. He who votes, is making decisions in political economy and is directing the Government. The solemn responsibility of intelligent men who neglect to even try to understand more of our system of national housekeeping, is a blot on our professed Christianity. We are not trying to do unto others as we wish to be done by. We too often vote and throw our influence with reckless ignorance. Our flag of distress is now flying and I most earnestly appeal to the people to come to the rescue.

The Storage of Silver Dollars.

Constant reference is being made concerning the great expense of the Government providing vault room for the storage of silver dollars. Although the silver dollar is sixteen times heavier than the gold dollar, it requires about twenty-seven times as much space for storage. Hence, the Government has been compelled to expend a few hundred thousand dollars for this purpose,—yet, how insignificant this expense appears when compared with the debts this coin assists to measure as well as pay. You might as well object to the expense of putting a door-knob on the entrance to your six thousand dollar residence. Much of this expense, however, is for the greater convenience of the people. As a general thing, the vault is the proper receptacle for all coin, while we demand well secured paper money for the pocket. Well secured paper money for general circulation is infinitely superior to the full legal tender coined money.

If you wished to pay a debt of a million dollars in coin, you can sling a bag containing 26 $\frac{886}{2240}$ tons of silver on your back and walk around the corner with it, just about as easily as to load yourself with 1 $\frac{1448}{2240}$ tons of gold coin. If you have to put it in carts,—we admit gold has a decided advantage. Our system of coin certificates puts these two kinds of money, on *an exact equality as to weight.* One of the principal reasons why the world has rated gold as worth about sixteen times as much as silver, is this decided superiority of gold over silver in handling it to make large payments, as well as in many of the minor transactions of life. A silver dollar in the Government vault, represented by a silver certificate circulating among the people, is doing its full duty all the time. To speak of these dollars thus in active duty—represented by the silver certificates in circulation, as useless dollars, is a very weak invention of the enemy.

The Gold "that nobody Wants."

It is officially reported that about 81 million of these much abused silver certificates which have been issued by the Government and are now represented by the silver dollars in our vaults found their way there simply because the level headed business men of the United States had 81 million dollars in gold coin in their hands, that was inconvenient to handle, and they requested the Treasury officials to issue silver certificates for it. This was done by the mildest kind of a twist of the laws and no one has been defrauded, yet the exchange was made dollar for dollar. To use a common phrase usually referred to silver "nobody wanted" this gold, and the poor old Government kindly took it out of pure generosity. The most of it was taken from New York merchants. Our merchants might have preferred gold certificates, but there were none to spare.

The New York Banks and Clearing-House and the Silver Certificates.

The New York Banks are very much afraid of our silver certificates, and the Treasury Department at Washington, by means of its connection with the New York Clearing-House, has unfortunately humored them in this fear. By the United States law of July 12, 1882, it is provided, that "no national banking association shall be a member of any clearing-house in which such (silver) certificates shall not be receivable in the settlement of clearing-house balances." This distinct law, made by the creators of the national banks, may yet be brought to bear, by the force of events or by public sentiment, on this clearing-house and on the banks—and show them that the nullification of our national laws is not a part of their chartered privileges. The people, when we join hands, cannot and will not be ruled by Wall Street. As a legislative body the New York Clearing-House is not recognized in the written Constitution of the United States. Custom does not make our laws, as under the unwritten Constitution of Great Britain. The very silly prank of the New York Clearing-House, as reported in their confidential circular issued on July 20, 1885, deserves a remark. In order to arrest the danger of receiving, as the law may compel, either silver certificates or silver dollars in the settlement of balances due them from the Government—they have *kindly* (?) resolved to loan the Government ten or twenty millions of their surplus gold and accept subsidiary silver coin in exchange. The light weight silver dollar is too heavy, but these subsidiary silver coins are about the right weight to suit their purpose. They anxiously call on all of the Banks throughout the country to help them in their efforts. The entire transaction reminds me of the brilliant financial sagacity of a seven year old child, who hearing his parents discuss the financial difficulties of housekeeping—proposed that his father should loan him a five dollar gold piece each Saturday morning and on Saturday night the boy would pay it into the family fund and thus assist his poor father. Such is the brilliancy of financiering urged by these gentlemen—who want to regulate the finances of the people of the United States! Our friend, Mr. Coe, he who suggested, in 1883, the brilliant expedient of *drowning* our silver dollars in the sea, is one of the signers of this circular. I hear that our Philadelphia Banks take no stock in this nonsense. Well may we ask does Wall Street or Congress make laws for the people!

Paper Money Statistics.

There is usually, a degree of importance placed on the amount of paper money in circulation that I have never been able to realize. The amount of paper money, strictly so-called, such as greenbacks and national bank notes, is so small, when compared with other forms of paper representative money, such as checks, drafts, bills of exchange, telegraphic and postal money orders and the other forms of circulating credit daily in use. The only important point to watch, seems to me to be, that these various kind of "*debts*" should never exceed the available assets. This paper money must have sound backing or it will have no more value than the leaves of the forest. Gold and silver full legal tender coin does the measuring, while these other forms of money are the much more active mediums of exchange.

Opposition of our National Banks to the Silver dollar and Certificates.

We have always regretted to observe the intense opposition of our National Banks to the silver coinage and to the silver certificates. We are glad to be able to credit these institutions as being of vast utility, both to the people and to the Government. They have done and are doing magnificent services for us. They should justly be fostered and maintained. They have probably fairly earned every cent received for many years from the special privileges, kindly granted them by the Government. A father may dearly love and admire his children, but when these children of the Government cry out with so much energy: stop the coinage of silver dollars; stop the issue of silver certificates!—melt up all of the first and recall all of the last!—we feel that their kind father, Uncle Sam, should pat them gently on the head and say: "Boys, have you not had your share of pie?" During the last session of Congress they made an active effort to obtain about 32 million more of a circulation of bank notes, based on their present supply of bonds. Should the monetary times get better, a sum like this judiciously loaned out, to their customers at interest, would be an item in their dividends well worth looking after. It is reported that there is about 63 million dollars of idle money, beyond the legal reserve, now in the vaults of the New York Banks. Under such circumstances, the entire sum, of new notes so vainly striven after last winter, would have been useless. The wealth, the business interests and the intelligence of the country are fully represented by our National Banks, and they feel the sad depression in our monetary affairs, keenly. They would give us national prosperity if it was in their power. Possibly, events may now be educating enough of their leaders in thought, so that more of them may see that their position on this silver question has not been a sound one; on the contrary, that it has been very *hostile to their own interests* as well as to those of the people.

In the last annual report of the Comptroller of the Currency, it is stated that the earnings of the 2664 National Banks was 3.66 per cent. on the capital and surplus for the six months ending September 1, 1884. If they were able to do as well for the next six months and make 7.32 per cent. per annum on their capital and surplus we would be pleased. Is it not probable, that this largely exceeds the average earnings of many other industries of the country during that same period, after paying the running expenses? Whatever may be decided to be the cause or causes of the present world-wide depression in business, the wealthy classes are most seriously affected by the loss of money due them as well as by the stoppage or decrease of dividends. The day laborer who is hunting around for work and who pleads for a fair day's pay, after the work is done, is not the only sufferer. The distress of the wealthy and leisure class of our people, encourages us to hope that they may utilize their leisure and supposed superior worldly wisdom in trying to find out the seat of the disease and assist in applying the proper remedies.

The Business Depression abroad.

In regard to the depression in business in other countries, we notice that Mr. George W. Cope, Secretary of the American Iron and Steel Association, states in his last annual report, that trade was much more unsatisfactory in 1884 throughout Europe than it was in 1883, and that during the early months of 1885, there was no change for the better; on the contrary, it was worse.

In Great Britain, in 1884, there was a marked reduction in the coal produced,—11 per cent. less pig iron was made—16 per cent. less steel, and a reduction of 42 per cent. is noted for iron and steel ship building. In the production of tin plates there was no reduction, rather a slight increase, but the price was the lowest on record. Reports from other sources, confirm this bad news concerning the great commercial and industrial depression, throughout the civilized world.

International Monetary Conference of 1881.

At the International Monetary Conference held at Paris in 1881, one of the United States Commissioners, the late ex-Postmaster-General Howe, said in his able speech defending bi-metallism: " that we seek a thrifty world, and it is our profound belief that no such world is possible if its money is limited to a single standard."

I do not intimate that a single standard has been adopted in Europe, but this attempt to adopt it is one of the leading causes for this unthrifty world, in which we as a nation are selling so much of our surplus products.

Another member, United States Senator, William M. Evarts, of New York, in speaking of the "unlucky incident," as he, happily calls the demonetization of our silver in 1873, spoke as follows concerning the necessity of the use of the two metals: "As there never had been a time in history when silver and gold had not been necessary and been used as money, or when their united strength was more than adequate for the unfolding progress of society, so above all things in this age and in the actual circumstances of the world was this true."

Ex-Senator Thurman, of Ohio, who was also one of the Commission, in his leading speech for bi-metallism, said: "I believe that bi-metallism will ultimately prevail; for I cannot see how the vast structure of credit, the most distinguishing feature of modern industry and commerce, can be supported on a gold basis alone." "With both metals, its base has often been found too narrow; but with one it would be, to my apprehension, positively unsafe."

Mr. S. Dana Horton, another delegate who was admitted to a seat, and who was also a delegate to the conference of 1878, contended most gallantly for bi-metallism. He has written an exceedingly able work, published in 1877, called *Silver and Gold*, published by Clark & Co., Cincinnati. In some mysterious way he arrived at the conclusion that we should not have remonetized silver until we had secured an international treaty as to the ratio we should use in our silver and gold coins, and had also secured the coöperation of the other leading nations of the world, in coinage. As an earnest student of his productions, and having a most profound admiration for his scholarship and abilities, yet I cannot see this question as he does. A ship may be launched in safety before she is ready for sea, and in fact the way to get her ready for sea is to put her afloat. We have a fair start, and have shown a good example to the world. We are only getting abreast of other nations in our domestic supply of silver coin while the bullion is cheaper. By our wise alteration in our law, in regard to the purchase of silver at market rates, the slight variation of ratio in the use of the two metals loses its old importance. In a very kind note from Mr. Horton, in 1884, he asks "what difference it would make to myself, if we should export all our silver, and coin gold alone?" This is the qestion I am trying to answer.

The Gresham Law.

About 300 years ago, an English gentleman, named Gresham, formulated a law that has taken his name, and has been pretty well executed, considering the length of time since the author has been gathered to his fathers. "Bad money will drive out good money," is a short way of stating this much quoted law. The meaning of the word "bad," as here applied to money, is that it must have less intrinsic value as bullion. We know, from the study of the monetary history of our country, that silver drove the gold out of our country previous to 1834, and that gold drove most of our silver out from that time to our greenback age, and then the greenbacks, representing so much less silver or gold than their face value, quickly learned the neat trick, and drove the gold and silver out of sight. Since March, 1878, we have been coining our very "bad" silver dollars at the rate of about 28 million a year, but the driving trick has been apparently lost. We have a large and influential class of men appealing to the ghost of Gresham, and anxiously asking why it does not appear.

We have shown you, by statistics officially prepared by those highest in authority, that the gold does not go, but that the amount has been increasing instead of diminishing. We have shown that, for the thirteen years immediately preceding our late war, we lost our gold at the rate of about 130 million dollars a year, yet we coined very little silver. It was not on account of the Gresham law, although the gold was then the "bad" money. We have shown that the Gresham law does not work in France, where the silver money is nearly three times as great in amount as in our country, and the gold largely exceeds our own. The silver money of France is about 3 per cent. worse in value when compared with their gold, than our silver is, when compared with our gold. What is the matter with the Gresham law? Why cannot our people see these events happening before their eyes, and take a little more practical education? The value of our silver dollar to the people as individuals, is not its bullion value, but is measured by what it may cost an individual to get this dollar. It will cost him, whether a foreigner or one of our citizens, just as much wheat, just as much cotton, just as much iron, or just as much of any of the products of labor, to obtain this dollar from the government mints, as to get the more valuable bullion gold dollar. Measured in this way, these coins are equal in value, and they fight out the battle on equal terms. The eminently wise provision put in the law of 1878, by that particularly clear-headed statesman, United States Senator Allison, of Iowa, compelling the government to buy all of the silver used in coinage, is the secret of this failure in the appearance of Gresham's ghost.

Allison is our Great Magician.

In course of time, should the bullion value of silver exceed the bullion value of gold, even to a part of the present ratio, and our coinage laws in regard to gold are not changed, the gold would pick up the driving trick, and we would quickly lose our silver. We hope by that time another Allison may be on hand to stop the game. Our silver producers cannot bring their silver to our mints, as they could at any time since their organization in 1792 up to 1873, and demand its coinage into dollars. They must take their chances, and sell their silver at market rates. This statement should make us see the base malice, falsehood, or ignorance, in saying that our silver coinage is only for the selfish personal benefit of the silver producer.

They, like any other industrious producer, profit by the demand for their product, but the special benefit and gain to the people from the silver coinage goes to our entire country.

If the coinage was stopped, we would expect the price of silver to fall rapidly, and our silver producers would suffer, but the people, the great producing class of our citizens, would suffer more in reduced prices for products and a further reduction in wages, and an increase in the value of debts.

Debts due England and Germany by other Nations.

In 1876, Mr. Seyd estimated that foreigners owed England about 5000 million dollars, and Germany about 2750 million dollars. Put it on wheels if you please, in ordinary carts, to get a glimpse of these sums. These two great creditor nations can insist, as a matter of selfish policy, in having these debts paid in the money of the highest intrinsic value. This may worry the debtors, but debts nearly always worry. The borrower has ever been the servant of the lender.

The hard creditor may easily put on such a high pressure, that the debtor abruptly squares accounts by bankruptcy.

This is becoming a very interesting feature of the discussion of this monetary revolution, by practical Englishmen, and by the metaphysical German.

The constant failure in the receipt of overdue debts and dividends, on what only a few years ago, were considered remarkably sound investments, are events that will educate England and Germany as no arguments possibly could. The clean-cut arguments of eminent European scholars, statesmen and financiers, such as Wolowski, Cernuschi, Rouland, Dumas, Seyd, Rusconi, Laveleye, and others, have fallen on dull ears,—but events will educate.

Practical Bi-metallism.

When the leading nations of the world do as we are now doing, go into the open market and buy the cheaper of the two metals, and cause it to be coined, by legislative demand, into full legal tender money, the old equilibrium between the intrinsic value of gold and silver will soon be reached, and practical bi-metallism, on a basis that other nations can accept, will be fully established. This will satisfactorily settle one of the most subtle and momentous questions of national housekeeping; give more equity to the contracts of paying an almost inconceivable mass of debts; steady the demand and price of labor, and of the products of labor, and tend to establish the financial world on a far sounder basis.

The question is one of such commanding importance, that it has received the closest attention of many of the most eminently wise and scientific minds of all civilized nations. As great as the question is in importance and in difficulty to understand, we most earnestly appeal to the mass of our clear-thinking people to settle it, as far as we, as a nation, are concerned. Part of it is easily within our grasp, and let us try and do our duty.

But remember we must all be armed with precise knowledge of the facts of the case, and of the United States laws.

The following table shows the amount of silver dollars actually owned by the government on the 1st of January of each year since their coinage; also, their value expressed in percentage, when compared with the net cash held by the government, and also the price paid at the beginning of each year for the pure bullion silver per ounce. On August 1, 1885, the price of pure silver at the U. S. Mint, Phila., was $1.07 per ounce.

This exhibit was presented officially by the Secretary of the Treasury on February 10, 1885, in obedience to a request from the House of Representatives. (See *Congressional Record*, Feb 12, 1885.)

A table of the number owned, percentage of value to the cost in the U. S. Treasury, and cost of the silver in the dollar, from 1879 to 1885.

Year.	Standard Silver Dollars actually owned by the U. S. Government on Jan. 1 of each year.	Their percentage compared with the net cash in the Treasury.	The cost of the pure silver per ounce at the beginning of each year.
1879	16,291,469	8.06	$1.0916
1880	29,343,812	13.19	1.1415
1881	12,002,807	5.61	1.1185
1882	7,274,617	3.09	1.1285
1883	25,573,182	11.43	1.0912
1884	22,731,664	8.98	1.1113
1885	31,636,954	13.21	1.0865

www.ingramcontent.com/pod-product-compliance
Lightning Source LLC
Chambersburg PA
CBHW020151170426
43199CB00010B/979